MADE IN LONDON

MADE IN LONDON
FROM WORKSHOPS TO FACTORIES

CARMEL KING &
MARK BREARLEY
Texts by CLARE DOWDY

MERRELL
LONDON · NEW YORK

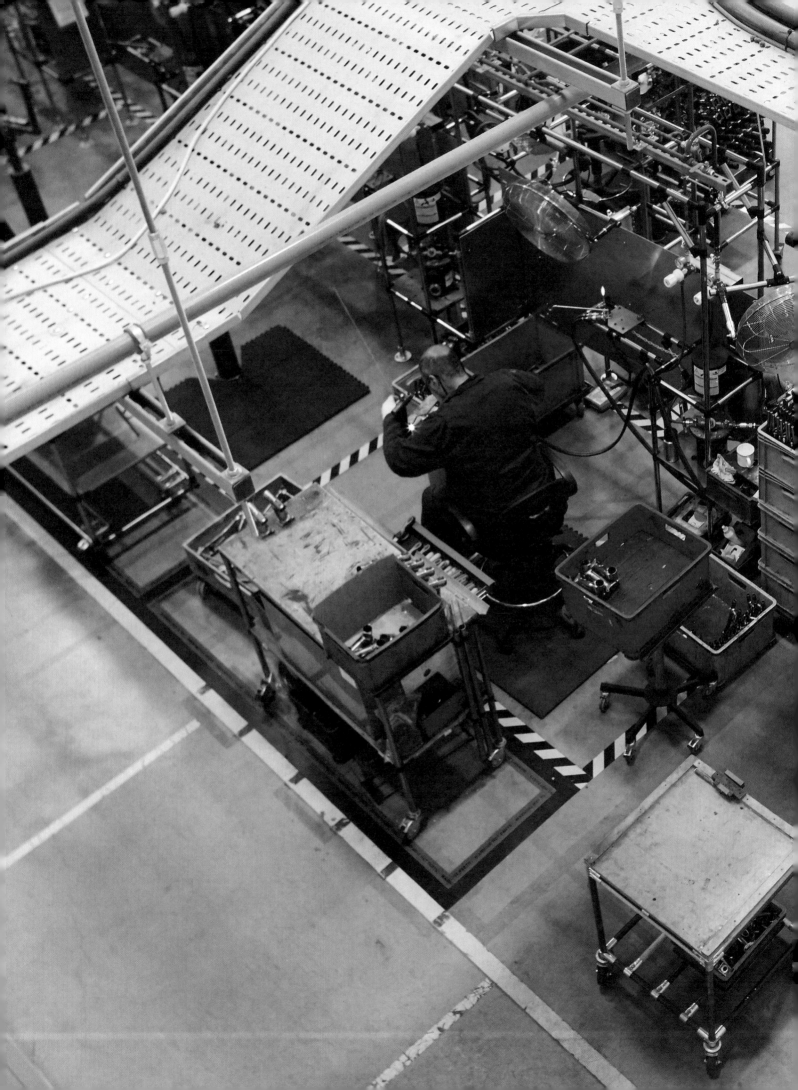

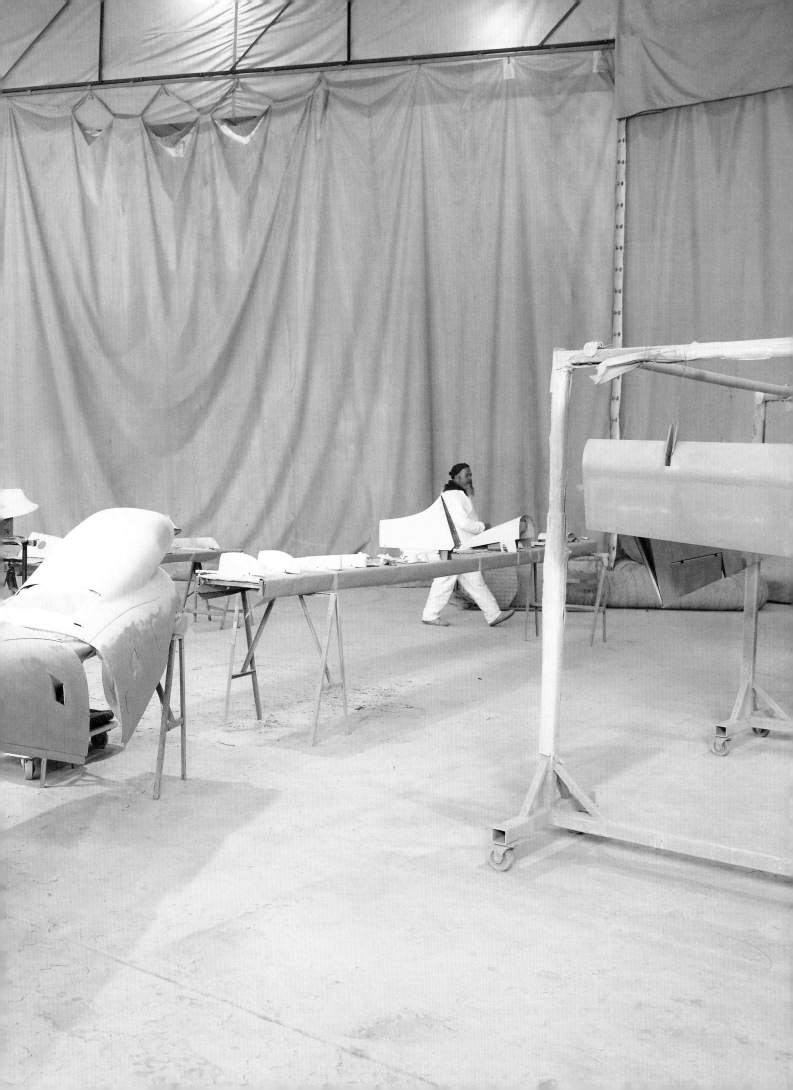

CONTENTS

INTRODUCTION
A Multitude of Minor Miracles

Mark Brearley

In 2011 I was lucky to land tickets for Trooping the Colour, London's annual ceremony marking the Queen's official birthday. From our seats in the spectator stands, the panorama included 1400 parading soldiers in dress uniform, 200 horses and 400 military musicians in massed bands. Eight weeks later, on 6 August, rioting started in Tottenham, north London. Over the following days, destructive expressions of discontent spread across the city.

As Head of Design for London, I was among the people from the Mayor of London's team sent to spend time where the trouble started, to become familiar with the area. In the following months, we pushed forward a detailed audit of the local economy, to capture an understanding and bring to light the specifics of businesses. The once-mighty industrial cluster in that part of town had declined during the previous decades, and the scars were evident. But by delving deeper, we discovered an impressively strong industrial scene, and noticed that long-established

My view of Trooping the Colour on a sunny day in central London in June 2011.

companies were being joined by thriving newer enterprises.

During the 1970s and on into the '80s, a shake-out of UK manufacturing had entrenched in the popular imagination an idea that factories had vanished and that 'we don't make things here any more'. I shared those cartoonish assumptions and, even while walking the streets of Tottenham, believed that London no longer produced anything. So, it was a surprise to discover that, interleaved with all the other industry, the logistics, the wholesalers and distributors, the depots and utilities facilities, there were more small manufacturers than you could shake a stick at. Among them, we came across Kashket & Partners, where sixty people produce the military dress uniforms I had seen paraded just weeks earlier, only a few miles away (pp. 30–33). Thousands of uniforms are meticulously handmade each year by the specialist tailors in Kashket's factory, minutes away from where those riots erupted. From there emerge gold coats for the State Trumpeters and the ceremonial uniforms of the Life Guards and the Blues and Royals of the Household Cavalry, and of the Gunners who fire the royal gun salutes.

Those manufacturers discovered while we walked the streets in 2011 made such an impression that in 2013 the exhibition *From Around Here* was organized to show off locally made items: garments, jersey fabric, shoes, leather goods, theatrical wigs, bread and cakes, furniture, mirrors, catering equipment, signs, architectural metalwork, carved stone and wood, all catching the eye through windows on Tottenham High Road. That is what set me off on the task of making a list of manufacturers in London today and of getting to understand the whole dynamic.

This book is part of that mission to unveil, explain and celebrate, to see whether perceptions can be changed and whether we can nurture a more encouraging and more welcoming attitude to a part of the economy that to me seems miraculous. My list is now heading towards 4000 businesses. While not definitive, it is the best there is, and the vitality and variety are breathtaking. Here I sketch out an overview and offer a few thoughts on what a good future could be like, and then you will see more about fifty such businesses – a taster of the manufacturing activity hidden away in the vastness of London.

Each of those fifty places of making has been photographed by Carmel King, while – after interviewing people at each business – Clare Dowdy has written the accompanying texts. I thank them both, and the brilliant team at Merrell Publishers, for an enjoyable and productive collaboration.

To delve deep into a metropolitan world of producers, it helps to be a producer yourself, and for me that happened by chance. In 2012 I went to buy a tray from a small urban manufacturer, and a few months later it had become a two-family business – my family and that of the founder. We make aluminium trays; about 25,000 per year emerge from our factory in Peckham. It started in the basement of a radio shop in the 1930s and became Kaymet in 1947, a classic story of city enterprise (pp. 110–13). But in 2013 the business nearly evaporated. Today we are on the up: we have more than tripled sales, grown the team to fourteen, and now export to forty countries.

Yet the storm clouds are above us. The local government that lords it over our area is driving ahead with the eradication of industry from around the Old Kent Road, where we are based; it wants large quantities of housing, and that requires clearances, a brush-aside

that threatens hundreds of businesses and several thousand jobs, and could eliminate manufacturing from another chunk of the city. The centrifuge in which we and our neighbours find ourselves is typical of today's London. As residential developments rise around us and the squeeze on space tightens, it is the right time for embattled urban producers to press for visibility, point out that *we are not nothing*, fight back through revelation and push for a shift of opinion. And so, I must send your mind on a journey.

Imagine catching a train from Fenchurch Street station heading towards Tilbury. Get off at Rainham, then walk across the marshes to the capital's eastern border and float up high, from where you gain a spectacular view that includes the snaking river and the distant towers of inner London. The scene takes in large chunks of industry, giant distribution sheds, packers and shippers, aggregate yards, bus garages, wharves with ships, stockholders and builders' merchants by the dozen, recycling facilities and water-treatment works, rail depots and terminals, and the site of the new Smithfield and Billingsgate markets. Nestling in this real-life diorama are a myriad of makers: Britvic, which makes Pepsi for London to drink; the rice miller Tilda; the Tate & Lyle sugar refinery (pp. 206–209); Whitaker & Sawyer, maker of paintbrushes; and Mason Pearson, crafter of

The rice miller and packer Tilda has been based in Rainham since 1988. Its site by the Thames allows ships to berth and unload rice directly into its silos.

Mason Pearson, manufacturer of world-renowned hairbrushes since 1885, moved to Rainham in 2009 when the business was required to vacate its factory in Stratford to make way for the development of facilities for the 2012 Olympic Games.

Top: The Ford Motor Company has been manufacturing in Dagenham, on its vast site by the Thames, since 1931. Today production is focused on engines, of which around fifty million have been made on this site.

Above: Each year at Veolia's Dagenham Plastics Facility some 300 million milk bottles are turned into 10,000 tonnes of high-quality food-grade HDPE pellets. The pellets are then made into new milk bottles, which are used in such big urban dairies as Freshways in Acton.

hairbrushes. In Belvedere there is bread-baking and vegetable and olive oil production. There are manufacturers of gold ingots, optical sorting machines, containers and cartons, taps and magnets; businesses working with metal, glass, paper and plastic; fabricators, turners, millers, punchers, platers and coaters. Alongside makers of windows, doors, wardrobes, kitchens, garden sheds, lifts and ducting are producers of pallets, laboratory glassware, heat exchangers, filler caps, wax, sausages, ice-cream wafers and smoked salmon.

From high up, you glimpsed parts of London's production economy. It had been written off, assumed to be in terminal decline, but has, in fact, returned to growth, alongside the rest of this large city's industry. According to the Greater London Authority, 11 per cent of jobs in London are offered by the industrial economy, work for close to half a million people, and producers are a vital slice of that employment.

Ford's diesel-engine plant in Dagenham, another part of the cityscape you looked over, is London's biggest factory, sending out more than one million engines each year. With a workforce of close to 2000, Ford Dagenham is in the process of focusing production on van engines while planning for the shift to fully electric. But Ford is now an eccentricity, the only maker in the capital employing over a thousand people. There are several factories, including the sugar refinery and some of the big bakeries, with teams of a few hundred, but the city's manufacturing economy is dominated by small businesses, and it is remarkably vigorous and diverse.

The majority of these businesses thrive by being tied to the London market and the everyday facilitation of our lives, making products – either as demand dictates or bespoke items – ranging from sandwiches and dairy products to metalwork and scenery. It is no small matter, this city-serving economy – humdrum and hidden, but essential. It must be close to the city it serves and must always be evolving, and it can be expected to expand strongly as the city's population continues to grow. In the future, Londoners will need many more than the 140-plus steel fabricators and at least 200 printers currently in existence, and there will be demand for additional wood workshops, multitudes of food and drink manufacturers, and much else besides.

Over the past three decades, some types of manufacturer in London – for example, in the fields of engineering and chemical products – have continued to contract or move away from the city. The haemorrhaging of process plants has included the likes of Allnex, Amylum, Guinness, Jablite, Kodak, Loders Croklaan, Murex, Pirelli, Pura, Sanofi and Sun Chemical. While it is likely that London will lose more of its few remaining big processors, it

Below: Camden Town Brewery started production in 2010, and by 2015 was brewing more than 200,000 pints per week. In 2017, supported by investment from its new owner, AB InBev, it established a 5400-square-metre (58,000 sq. ft) brewery in Ponders End.

Bottom: Set up in Harringay in 2014, the Albion Knitting Company was the first industrial-scale fully fashioned flat knitter to be established in the capital in eighty years. Today it makes up to 6000 knitted garments per month for Paul Smith, Givenchy, Chloé, Chanel and other luxury brands that appreciate having both sampling and production in London.

appears that such structural loss, a century-long process of dispersal, has nearly run its course. The final shake-out is now balanced by a surprising return to growth across several manufacturing sectors.

When Nestlé shut down its coffee factory in Hayes in 2015, it shed 230 jobs, and the closure soon after of AB InBev's Stag Brewery in Mortlake resulted in 180 redundancies. But the rapid emergence of small coffee roasteries looks set easily to compensate for the loss of Nestlé. Similarly, while at one time it seemed likely that London would become a one-brewery city (Fuller's in Chiswick), in just a decade more than seventy new breweries have emerged, and a handful – among them Meantime (pp. 210–13), Camden Town and Fourpure – have upscaled production dramatically. The jobs generated thus far by the new breweries greatly exceed the loss of employment from AB InBev in Mortlake.

Today baking is rampant; it is one of those fast-growing, just-in-time urban production industries. High-volume bakers such as Warburtons, Hovis, Greggs and Allied have all expanded their London facilities. Warburtons in Brimsdown is particularly impressive: £70 million has been invested in the plant over the past decade, and it now runs round the clock, making 23,000 loaves per hour, over three million items per week; some 300 people are employed there. As a result of the blossoming appetite for artisan bread, the number of smaller wholesale bakeries has increased, to about 170 at present. Brands such as Konditor, Paul, Honeyrose, Ladurée and Blackbird have all become significant London producers.

In fact, food manufacture has been the quickest to evolve, capitalizing on the strength it has long gained from a culturally diverse population. As well as an abundance

of craft breweries and coffee roasteries, London now has eighteen distilleries and eight soft-drink producers, most of them new. Chocolate-making is booming, and the city also hosts a huge number of niche food-preparation and catering businesses that include high-volume makers of ready meals, sustained by the phenomenal growth of air and rail travel via London.

The expansion trends have been accelerated by increasing prosperity and by an interest in products of local origin. For example, the bespoke tailoring industry has reversed many decades of decline, and the city now boasts well over 100 such businesses – believed to be the world's greatest concentration. That includes our uniform-making acquaintances at Kashket and the remarkable cluster that continues to thrive in central London.

A few years ago, the city's broader garment-manufacturing capabilities were a mere residue of a once-formidable sector. In 1938, in inner London alone, there were more than 14,000 clothing factories employing 178,000 people. But seventy years later, the entire London garment industry had shrunk so dramatically that it seemed to be heading for oblivion. However, over the past decade, the vibrant design scene, with its associated network of samplers and pattern cutters, and the skills in the few remaining legacy producers have provided a fertile base for growth. Clothing brands have been the fastest to recognize that the label 'made in London' is a major asset. Production volumes are increasing at a fast pace, and today there are more than 300 clothing workrooms and factories, including thirty-five making shoes.

While the production of military dress uniforms in Tottenham might once have been judged as quirky, such meticulous capabilities can today be understood as an indicator of London's potential for manufacturing growth. The same can be said of the survival of three metal spinners, three paint producers, four mannequin manufacturers, six gunmakers, a dozen foundries, fifteen lift fabricators and sixty-five precision-engineering workshops, alongside makers of umbrellas, ceremonial hats, briar pipes, French

horns, guitars and violins, go-karts, radars, instrument cases, picture-framing machines, lights, electron tubes, clocks, alternators, ladders, tipper-truck bodies, scaffold towers, staging, coin-slide mechanisms, propshafts, paper bags, cheese slicers, solenoids, gas springs, music stands, traction sheaves and snooker cues.

The growing number of people in London interested in luxury – who in many cases have a high level of technical or creative skill, combined with a go-getting drive and a love of the urban lifestyle – is also having an energizing effect on making in the city. Dunhill, W&H Gidden and Tanner Krolle were formerly among the few surviving own-brand luxury leather goods producers in London, and they seemed anachronistic. But now each is reviving and repositioning, and they have been joined by at least seventy newer makers such as Bill Amberg Studio, Thomas Lyte, Frank Horn, Alfie Douglas and Serran. This phenomenon repeats across many manufacturing categories that are flourishing

Right, top: A White Spot shell briar bent billiard pipe with sterling-silver band, produced in Alfred Dunhill's Walthamstow workshop.

Right: A Model 45 Heritage descant horn, made by Paxman Musical Instruments in its factory in Long Lane, Bermondsey.

not just because of the London market for specialist and deluxe goods (which could be served from elsewhere) but also because the people with the desire and the skill to produce want to be in this city.

New enthusiasm for making has bubbled up; it is another cause of the strengthening production dynamic in many mature cities. No one predicted the blossoming of urban wooden-spoon carvers, and while this may seem bizarre, it points to a broader trend. In London, craft-making by many microbusinesses has become, once again, a hefty component of the manufacturing economy. Jewellery and other fine metalwork had continued to play a significant role in this economy, partly on account of the impressive throng of jewellers in the Hatton Garden area, but recently the sector has been vaulting ahead thanks to many dozens of new workshops. Small-scale production of ceramics and treen, as well as scents and candles, is expanding. The making of art, dominated by printmaking and painting, has grown exponentially, and while some art emerges from a handful of factory-scale studios, most comes from many hundreds of mini-producers, the city's most prodigious cottage industry. Open-access workshops have been helping the popularization of making, with more than fifty springing up across the city in recent years. Some are now on a substantial scale, such as Bloqs in Edmonton, which has recently grown to fill a new 3000-square-metre (32,000 sq. ft) building, with facilities for working with wood, metal and fabric.

And then there are global shifts that have given a further boost to the refresh of making. Many people have fond childhood memories of painting plastic models with Humbrol enamel paint in tinlets. The paints were long made in Hull, then for a time in China. Now they are made by Rustins in its small factory in Cricklewood. This is part of a major swing to reshore, to localize some production, and several of London's specialist makers are benefiting.

London manufacturers within numerous niches are thriving: Caterham® conjures sports cars, Brompton fashions folding bicycles (pp. 66–69), and Hensoldt UK makes navigation and surveillance systems. Furniture production, which seemed doomed just a few years ago, is flourishing once again, with around 230 bespoke and small-batch makers. Perhaps the sector with the most remarkable success story is film production, which is currently experiencing dramatic growth. The city has long had one of the world's most successful theatre and events sectors, supporting over forty set, scenery and propmaking businesses, as well as wig and costume producers. Indeed, the two biggest places of making in central London are the backstage workshops of the National Theatre and the Royal Opera House (pp. 132–35). Now much of that same capability is both facilitating the film-industry boom and advancing alongside it. London and the surrounding areas presently boast an estimated 200 sound stages, and new film studios are emerging at a staggering pace. During this upsurge such specialists as Mo-Sys, a Greenwich-based deviser and manufacturer of camera robotics and virtual film-production technologies, have emerged and prospered.

In 2015 I spent some time in Belfast. Three thousand people work in Spirit AeroSystems' aircraft-wing factory, which looms large on the horizon when you land at the city's airport. The business began in London in 1903 as Short Brothers, and initially made hot-air balloons in railway arches next to Battersea

A tinlet of Humbrol enamel paint made in north-west London by Rustins. Production was relocated from China in 2012 after a contract-producer search by the brand owner, Hornby Hobbies.

Above: From the 1950s onwards, Hawker Aircraft produced 957 Hawker Hunter jet fighters at its factory in Ham, near Richmond upon Thames. Other London-grown companies that have played a significant role in the history of the UK aerospace industry include Sopwith, Short Brothers, Handley Page, de Havilland, Fairey, Airco, Plessey, Decca Radar, Smiths and Racal.

Below: Caterham® has produced the Seven, a lively little two-seater sports car, since 1973. Several hundred emerge each year from the factory in Slade Green, just inside London's south-eastern boundary.

gasworks; a few years later it became the world's first series aircraft manufacturer. Many other famous names from the evolution of the UK aerospace industry emerged from the city, as did the car companies Vauxhall, Lotus, Aston Martin and Bentley. Hundreds of other manufacturer out-migration stories can be traced, in history and the present.

With its formidable concentration of resources and strong entrepreneurial dynamic, London continues to be a surprisingly abundant seedbed of manufacturing. Through the incubation and growth cycle that each enterprise rides, a proportion of companies will decide to stay in the city, while others scatter. This dispersion nourishes the economy with energetic and evolving businesses across a geography far beyond the metropolitan area. But what is painful to observe is that now, more than ever before, a large number of producers leave through force, rather than go voluntarily; the diaspora arises less out of choice than out of someone else's desire to grab the businesses' place in the city.

I first noticed those storm clouds above the Old Kent Road, and now, beneath them, across London, all-conquering housing growth is reducing the capital's capacity to welcome a varied economy. Industrial businesses, both existing and emerging, are being expelled as we race towards a shortage of suitable accommodation measuring in at some 700 hectares (1730 acres), according to the city government's own figures. If the process is not halted, then our economy and

culture will become less diverse and thus less resilient; there will be a shrunken range of jobs available, and we could stifle swathes of fruitfulness.

This book is a revelation of renewed vigour, of a surprising return to London manufacturing growth. That is the easy strand. But also told here is a tale of robust businesses, the workers of many minor miracles, confronted by developer and local government hostility, and forced to divert their energies into fighting expulsion from their city. The sweep-away process is clumsy, and fighting it now eats up hefty chunks of many producers' time. I know of plenty who have been relentlessly cajoled and are experiencing dramatic rent increases, while others have endured expropriation action and intimidation. It is a rough battle, and right now it looks like a hard one to win.

Yet the planners, who allowed this problem to emerge, have been looking the other way. In London we have a city plan still mired in old ideas about the geography of the economy. It implies that just a handful of consolidated and segregated large industrial estates will be sufficient. It encourages the erasure of hundreds of smaller working areas, and fails to acknowledge that industrial uses are remarkably varied and operate at many scales. There is little mention in that plan (the London Plan

2021) of the differing relationships between productive activity, the people driving businesses forward and the markets served.

A good city has industry – not hidden away, but present and accepted. Such a city can accommodate the messy as well as the neat; it can make room for distributors, repairers and recyclers, and can host small makers and producer start-ups as well as established manufacturers. A better London would be proud of its multitude of small factories and its many midsized ones; it would let us see all this enterprise as we walk by, and those businesses would be appreciated and respected as much as the schools and shops, the places where we gather and take our leisure, the offices, healthcare facilities and eateries. That future city would make space for all the ventures to which people give life, as well as for the practical, just-in-time essentials that support daily lives. That place would have not only large-scale industrial areas that are woven into the city's continuity, but also a filigree of premises across the entire capital. Each of London's 600 high-street localities could include space suitable for smaller industry, for modest-scale workshops, workrooms, storerooms, depots and yards, as part of

its mix. Industrial premises suitable for London's businesses should become a component of more new developments; and we must evolve our building types and configurations, and devise new ways of incorporation into a city that is becoming ever more intensely occupied.

Cities are the home of innovation and enterprise, a great crucible of the new, and that includes making. We should further reveal what we have and work to win people round, while at the same time pushing the policy- and decision-makers to recognize that manufacturing is a vital part of metropolitan life, one that should be visible, understood and nurtured, so that its momentum can be sustained. Now is the right time to embrace production in London, to realize that we need it, shout out that we want it, and act to sustain a welcome for the world of wonders celebrated in this book.

Left: The Vent-Axia Standard Range extractor fan, launched by the market-leading company in 1961, when it moved to Crawley from Putney, where it had been based since 1936. Other manufacturers that were originally based in London include Royal Doulton in Stoke-on-Trent, Charbonnel et Walker in Dorchester, Trebor in Sheffield, Swizzels in New Mills, Ambala in Welwyn Garden City, Sarson's in Middleton, Costa Coffee in Basildon, Gratnells in Harlow, Hille in Ebbw Vale, Vitsœ in Leamington Spa and Kent Brushes in Apsley.

Below: The totemic yellow model of Matthew Gregorowski's factory and house – created in 2016 for a student design project at London Metropolitan University – provides a simple reminder of an objective and a challenge to many decades of assumptions about the segregation of activities and the distancing of industry.

CLOTHING
& SHOES

Blackhorse Lane Ateliers
Denim garments

Walthamstow
blackhorselane.com

Han Ates's family has deep roots in the textile industry. A second-generation Londoner with Turkish-Kurdish ancestry, Ates set up his first tailoring business in Blackhorse Lane, Walthamstow, in 1996. In 2015 he established Blackhorse Lane Ateliers (BLA) in the same building, a renovated 1920s factory with high ceilings and big windows. He also operates a shop in Coal Drops Yard, King's Cross, which brings his staff total to twenty-two.

Every year BLA's workshop staff make 10,000 pairs of ready-to-wear jeans from selvedge (high-quality denim woven on an old-fashioned shuttle loom) and organic raw denim. 'We offer a lifetime repair policy that discourages fast fashion', Ates explains.

The team researches traditional manufacturing techniques and combines them with tailoring rules, which dictate that garments must be beautiful both inside and out. An example is their 'one-piece fly' construction. Patented in 1887, it was discovered by the team in a denim archive. 'Over the years, this original construction was eradicated in favour of faster and more efficient construction methods, but to us it represented a clean, durable, crafted finish, one worth reinstating in our jeans', says Ates. Like some others, he was dissatisfied with the quality of mass-produced jeans: 'Denim jeans are a heritage product, a seasonless staple garment with a 150-year history.'

Ates and BLA are part of a rapid revival of tailoring and garment production in London in recent years. There are a substantial number of other new and established businesses of this type, and they are growing fast.

As a Londoner, Ates feels that he has two heritages: 'my cultural heritage and my professional heritage'. The business is in the capital because 'this is my home, on a personal and professional level. In a sense, I want to give back to London through BLA.' Being in London is also good for business because it is 'full of creative, like-minded people, a situation that creates so many opportunities for collaboration, knowledge exchange and building community among makers'.

This sense of community-building and collaboration can be seen in the workshop's open-door policy. It has led to a steady flow of pop-up events attracting students, tutors, designers, brands and local residents.

The team at Blackhorse Lane Ateliers, twenty-two members strong, favours rigid (non-washed) denim. As it is worn, the wearer imprints their own body shape into the garment.

Han Ates, founder of Blackhorse Lane Ateliers, is inspired by the European tailors of the past who migrated to the United States and made jeans to order.

The business produces ready-to-wear jeans and also offers a made-to-measure service, where customers can choose their fabric and trims.

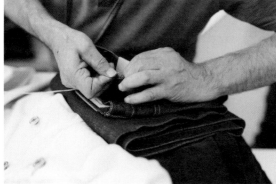

Kenan Habali (below, left), manager of the 3800-square-metre (41,000 sq. ft) factory, has been in the business for more than forty years and with Blackhorse Lane Ateliers for the past seven years.

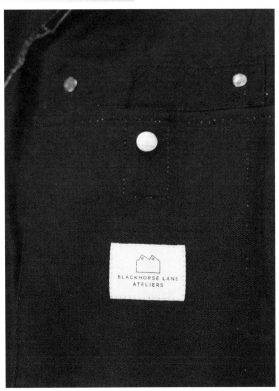

Freed of London
Ballet and dance shoes

Hackney
freedoflondon.com

Freed of London is the only company in the world that handmakes *pointe* shoes for the mass market, available off the shelf. It also custom-makes shoes for individual dancers, and its first famous customer was the prima ballerina Dame Margot Fonteyn.

Frederick Freed, a cobbler, and his milliner wife, Dora, opened their Covent Garden shop in 1929. At that time, *pointe* shoes were all the same width. Fonteyn was lured in by Frederick's sign offering to make a shoe to fit the ballerina, rather than the ballerina having to fit the shoe.

Freed's main production site has been in Well Street in Hackney since the 1970s. There, its eighty members of staff include twelve makers, some of whom have been with the company for forty years; one employee, Sadie (who does stitching), met Dora Freed when she was a youngster almost fifty years ago.

When the Freeds retired in 1968, Leicester man D.H. Sam Thompson bought the company, and some production is still carried out there. Freed's *pointe* shoemakers in London and Leicester together produce 250,000 Classic pairs a year, with each maker able to produce around forty pairs a day.

The construction and fit vary slightly from maker to maker. Each maker has their own symbol, which they are given when they start at Freed, and each is assigned their ballerinas, who generally stay with them throughout their dancing careers.

Sophie Simpson, senior manager of retail and ballet company sales, says of the capital: 'It's the home of UK ballet. A lot of ballet schools and ballet companies are based here, and it's convenient for customers.' But she admits that the team discuss their London location on a weekly basis: 'We'd be silly if we didn't. Every manufacturer has to look at what else is going on.'

The company's shoes have been worn in countless productions, including the opening and closing ceremonies of the London Olympic Games in 2012. Freed also made Natalie Portman's shoes for the film *Black Swan*.

Next to the *pointe*-shoe workshop is a bigger workshop where ballroom, Latin, tap, character and stage shoes are made.

In 1993 the business was sold to the large Japanese retail company Onward Kashiyama, which allowed Freed to continue with its traditional manufacturing methods. 'They've greatly expanded the name of Freed of London overseas in Asian and US markets,' says Simpson, 'and they've helped us expand our ballroom and Latin collections.'

The hard block on the toe of a *pointe* shoe is built up with paste and layers of hessian and card to a dancer's specification. The shoes are put in an oven overnight at 80°C, to harden the paste.

The *pointe* shoes are made inside out on a last (the turn-shoe method). The sole is stitched to the upper and then the shoe is turned right side out.

Freed of London was the
first manufacturer in the
UK to produce skin-tone
pointe shoes for dancers.

Kashket & Partners
Military dress uniforms

Tottenham
firminhouse.com/about-us/kashket-partners/

Beefeaters, colonels and royalty get their ceremonial and parade uniforms from an industrial site in Tottenham. The 1960s building, which rubs shoulders with a carpet warehouse and a taxi rank, was originally – and coincidentally – used for the manufacture of Marks & Spencer's suits. Nowadays, the factory makes more than 5000 bespoke items a year, from scarlet tunics and riding breeches to ladies' regimental ball gowns.

The building is the home of Kashket, which describes itself as Europe's biggest bespoke tailoring factory that handmakes from scratch. There is some competition from Savile Row, 'but we are bigger', says Nathan Kashket.

The fourth-generation business was started by Alfred Kashket, a Russian milliner who made felt hats for Tsar Nicholas II. He fled to England as a political refugee in the 1920s and resumed tailoring. Kashket & Partners was founded in 1951. Alfred's son, master tailor Bernard Kashket, MBE, is chairman; his grandson, senior master tailor Russell Kashket, is managing director; his great-grandson Nathan is the contract manager and production planner.

The company moved from Hoxton to bigger premises in 2004. When customers visit to be measured, they get a shock when they pass through the office and 'the skinny hallway into the big factory', says Nathan. In the brightly lit open-plan space, there is sewing, steaming and pattern-cutting. Nathan points out, 'It takes years and years to become a master pattern cutter.' Another highly skilled group are the hand-sewers, known as Felling Hands. Kashket is one of the last tailors that still embroiders in-house, Nathan adds.

Among the sixty factory staff are three married couples and one mother and son. Some staff are very long-standing, among

Three generations of Kashkets are involved in the business (from left): Marlon, head of production; Bernard, chairman; Nathan, contract manager and production planner; and Russell, managing director.

them the production manager, head cutter and head of trouser production, who have been with the company twenty-two, twenty-three and thirty-six years respectively.

Kashket's London address is important for business. 'The Ministry of Defence requires us to be no more than 30 miles from Wellington Barracks, in case of emergencies', Nathan explains. Growth continues, and, in order to increase its bespoke tailoring, the company plans to lease a second factory, also in London if possible.

Nathan, who is as well turned out as his clientele, stresses that whatever their rank and the colour of their blood, each customer is treated with the same respect.

The military buttons and insignia that go on the uniforms are made by Firmin & Sons, a Birmingham-based company bought by Kashket in 2006.

Embroidering starts with the artisan hand-drawing braid on to cloth. 'Because each person in the Army is a different size, we must make the braiding in proportion', explains Nathan Kashket.

Kashket made the wedding uniforms for Prince William, Duke of Cambridge and Prince Harry, Duke of Sussex.

Carréducker
Hand-sewn shoes

South Bank
carreducker.com

Some years after completing apprenticeships in hand-sewn shoemaking, Deborah Carré and James Ducker wanted a challenge. 'We thought we could be successful as a bespoke shoemaking company', says Ducker. In 2004 they founded Carréducker at Cockpit Arts studios in Bloomsbury with the aim of changing the perception of their craft and teaching the technique. 'We felt the trade would die out or stay niche if we didn't train other makers', explains Carré. She is also a trustee of the Queen Elizabeth Scholarship Trust, which supports the training of aspiring craftspeople.

Carré adds that, through the firm's evening classes, 'we've been quite instrumental in changing access to the industry'. There is now a growth in independent makers of hand-sewn shoes, and of the scattering of such operators in London, two attended their classes.

These classes, which took place at Carréducker's Shoreditch address, continue at the new first-floor, two-room studio at the back of the Oxo Tower. There, the duo, who enjoy bantering and share a good sense of humour, make the shoes themselves. They use pieceworkers – some based in London – to carry out tasks such as creating patterns and stitching the uppers. Demand fluctuates, but they have the capacity to make fifty pairs a year.

Carré and Ducker both live in the capital and say the location of their studio is good for students and for their many overseas customers: 'When they're passing through London, they stop off and see their tailor and shoemaker', says Ducker. They also operate a shoemaking service at the flagship Gieves & Hawkes store in Savile Row.

However, Carré points out that London is a competitive environment: 'We feel we're one of the city's genuine craft-based businesses. But it's a challenge to be above the noise of everyone else pushing authenticity and craft.'

In recent times, Carréducker has developed a virtual foot-measuring kit for people who cannot or do not want to travel. And the company has expanded its range: alongside bespoke hand-sewn shoes, it now offers bespoke manufactured pairs, which require less hand-sewing. 'Until recently, we made what we were trained to do: classic English hand-welted shoes', says Ducker. 'But leather-soled shoes are quite formal and structured. Nowadays, with the general trend towards trainers, customers want a softer, casual shoe.'

As well as growing the business, the duo want to 'continue our outreach as ambassadors for the craft of hand-sewn shoemaking'. As Carré explains, that includes creating more video content for remote learners; travelling globally to deliver masterclasses and creating experiential events at hotels, as modules on fashion and footwear courses; and continuing to expand their training programme in London.

Deborah Carré and James Ducker stand on the steps outside the apartment block off City Road where their former basement workshop was housed. In spring 2022 they moved to a new workspace in Oxo Tower Wharf, South Bank.

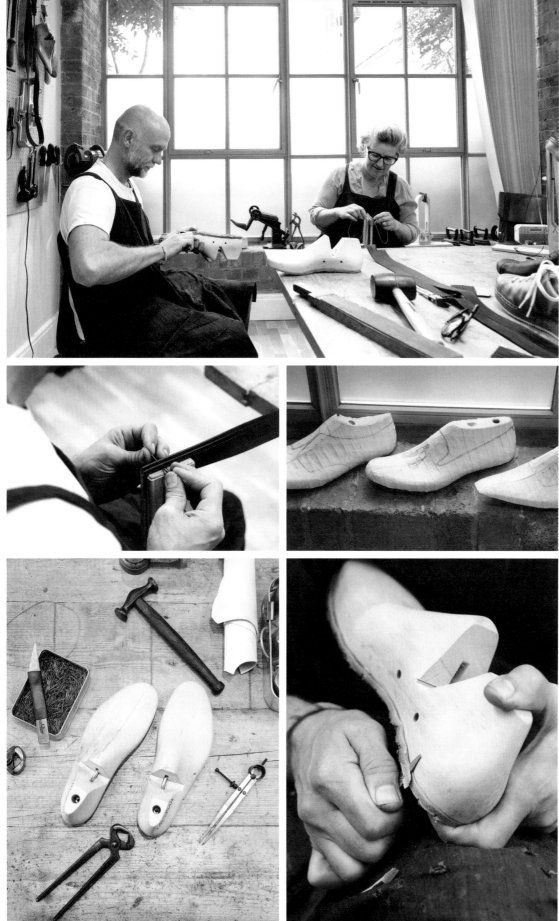

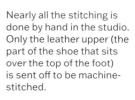

Nearly all the stitching is done by hand in the studio. Only the leather upper (the part of the shoe that sits over the top of the foot) is sent off to be machine-stitched.

Customer fittings at the Shoreditch address took place in the bespoke shoe room, where lasts – the wooden shoe models that are produced to order – hung in clusters from the ceiling, each inscribed with the customer's name.

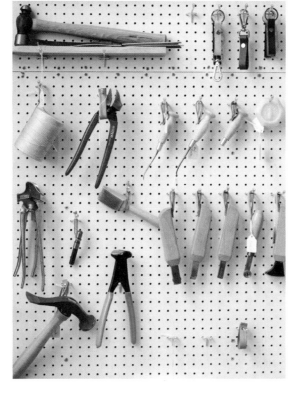

The Shoreditch studio had a teaching space: a large room with traditional hand tools on pegboards and a big worktable for students. The South Bank studio is similarly kitted out.

Hand & Lock
Embroidery

Fitzrovia
handembroidery.com

Hand & Lock is able to trace its roots back to 1767, when a young French Huguenot refugee, M. Hand (first name unknown), fled to London and started manufacturing and selling lace to military tailors. He expanded into the design and manufacture of military badges and uniform accoutrements for officers' dress uniforms.

Around 200 years later, in 1956, the embroidery designer Stanley Lock took over his employer's embroidery house on his retirement, renaming it S. Lock Ltd. Clients included such couturiers as Christian Dior, Norman Hartnell and Hardy Amies, who made gowns for the Queen and Queen Mother. In 1981 the company worked with David and Elizabeth Emanuel on Princess Diana's wedding veil.

In 2001 the firms merged to form Hand & Lock. The company's two adjacent buildings

in the West End are surrounded by offices and furniture showrooms. While hand-embroidering techniques have changed little since M. Hand's time, clients now include up-and-coming fashion designers, interior designers, PR companies and costume designers for theatre, film and television.

One building on Margaret Street houses the craft. In the main hand-embroidery room, half a dozen studio staff cut, iron and embroider fabric. Beyond that is the digital-machine department, which is growing because digitally created embroidery is popular with film and TV costume departments. Also in this building, Hand & Lock's shop sells embroidery materials, such as the goldwork bullion for which the company is famous, and military laces and badges.

The production director, Jessica Pile, who started as an intern in 2010, describes the process: 'A client approaches Hand & Lock with an idea. A designer works on the embroidery design and annotates the agreed design for embroidery. Based on the designer's notes, an embroiderer actions the embroidery.' A small badge takes about sixteen hours to make.

There are many small-scale machine embroiderers in the capital, but only three hand-embroidery companies. And of those, 'we're the longest-standing and biggest in terms of staff and turnover, I assume', says Pile.

Since becoming production director in 2014, Pile has tried to streamline the thirteen-strong business: 'We've grown over the last ten years, which is why we're higgledy-piggledy over two buildings.' The company has considered moving out of town, 'but we've never been willing to take the risk'. Its central location makes it accessible to visiting customers, and it is easy for makers to nip out and source products such as ribbon.

Alice Murrell, production manager (in front), and Jasmine Ataç, studio manager of Hand & Lock, which specializes in ancient and modern embroidery techniques.

The company has 250 years' experience embellishing, embroidering and monogramming garments for the Royal Family, the military and such fashion houses as Dior, Hermès and Louis Vuitton.

Opposite: Hand & Lock's design methods and hand-embroidery techniques have changed very little since 1767. Depending on the needs of the client, the embroidery can be subtle or very bold.

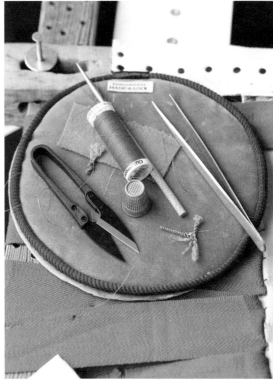

The Hand & Lock team offers classes around the world, teaching traditional embroidery skills while promoting quality British craftsmanship.

PRACTICAL EQUIPMENT

James Ince Umbrellas
Umbrellas

Bethnal Green
inceumbrellas.co.uk

Why the Ince family started making umbrellas in 1805 is 'lost in the mists of time', says Clare McCammont, business and civil partner of Richard Ince, a sixth-generation umbrella-maker. For the Inces, who were tailors, umbrellas were probably a sideline, since they already had the cutting and stitching skills.

The nine-strong company now makes around 17,000 umbrellas a year in its workshop in Bethnal Green's iconic Vyner Street, near its original site in Spitalfields. The two-storey workshop is in an industrial street, although, as McCammont explains, 'We've lost most of the other makers around us, because the buildings are being turned into residential. It's more coffee shops and art galleries now.'

The Inces moved from Suffolk to London for trade and skills. Historically, they sold mostly to city gents. Then, in the umbrella's late Victorian heyday, gentlefolk would promenade with parasols and walking umbrellas. Nowadays, around 70 per cent of Ince umbrellas go to central London retailers. 'We rely on skilled workers', says McCammont. 'Our team all live locally, so we couldn't move out.' To increase its stock of skilled workers, the company is training a young man from scratch as a fabric cutter through the government's Kickstart Scheme.

Each job starts on the long cutting bench, where triangles of fabric are cut out. The pieces are carried upstairs to a machinist, who sews them together to create a canopy. The machinist then makes a thin strap, with a button or popper, and attaches it to the canopy. Meanwhile, on the ground floor, the frame-maker makes a frame with a wooden or metal shaft and eight metal ribs. Tips are attached to the corners of the canopy as it is secured to the frame, and once it has been tied to the middle of each rib, the canopy is ironed and rolled. The last part to be fitted is the handle.

The oldest umbrella-maker in the UK has survived because, as Ince says, 'we've multiple irons in the fire. That's allowed us to pivot and gear our activities to what was in vogue at the time, and supply different industries.' That could be extra-big or specially designed umbrellas for welders on the railways or for hotel doormen, newspaper vendors and bookmakers. The firm also makes one-offs for film, TV and theatre, such as the Netflix adaptation of *Rebecca* and Samuel Beckett's play *Happy Days*, in which a James Ince umbrella burst into flames on the London stage every night. And Ince explains that, for *Paddington 2*, 'we made the parasols in the wonderfully camp finale with Hugh Grant having a whale of a time'.

Historically, James Ince Umbrellas has been the umbrella propmaker of choice for Disney and Warner Bros., and the company supplies *Mary Poppins* stage productions around the world.

Richard Ince learnt the trade from the company's skilled artisans when he was a teenager. He took over the business and became managing director in 1998.

James Ince Umbrellas relies on skilled workers, all of whom live locally. Around 10 per cent of the umbrellas are exported.

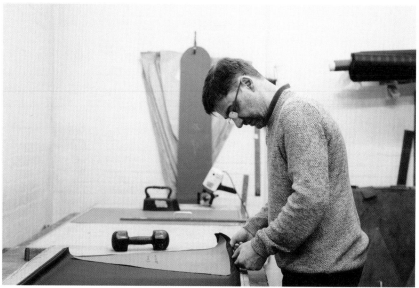

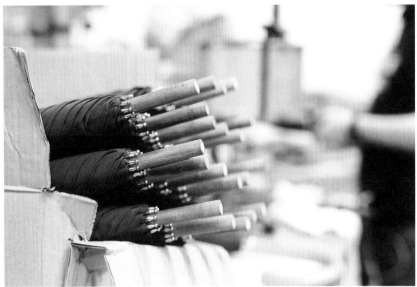

The company makes large umbrellas specially designed to fit in clamps on railways, so that tracks do not get wet when they are being welded together.

Barber Wilsons & Co.
Taps

Wood Green
barberwilsons.com

When the property developer Jeremy Bigland heard that the premises of Barber Wilsons & Co. were for sale, he was initially interested in the site as a potential residential project. But when he visited London's oldest tap factory, he changed his mind: 'I thought it would be a crying shame to see the business break up and dissolve. We owed it to the family members and staff who put in all the hard work to keep the business going there.' So Bigland and his business partner, Andy Warren, bought the company in 2018 from the third-generation Wilsons.

In 1899 brothers William and Walter Wilson started making taps and valves, and in 1905 they were joined by Edward Barber. During the First World War they made shell noses and fuses. The construction boom after the Second World War led to their taps being in high demand. In more recent years, the company has supplied brassware for hotels, including The Connaught, The Grosvenor and Four Seasons Hotels and Resorts, as well as for the Royal Household.

Barber Wilsons is on a small industrial site, next to a taxi-repair centre that is due to be replaced by twenty-nine residential units. 'On a weekly basis, we get letters from developers trying to buy our site', says Bigland. But he is adamant that the business is not going anywhere: 'For me, it was important to keep the heritage of the company, in London, alive.'

The firm is still in its original 1905 building in Crawley Road, Wood Green, with Crittall windows and old pastel-green lettering spelling out the company name. Inside, there are old casts and wooden moulds and a historic polishing machine. During the Second World War, when coal was scarce, the owners allowed workers to take up the factory's oak parquet flooring to burn as fuel at home. Patches of parquet remain where the heavy machinery stood.

Of Barber Wilsons's twenty-five London staff, ten are in production. The oldest employee – the head machinist, who works with manual lathes – turns eighty-one in 2022. 'It's been his life', Bigland says. Casting is done in the Midlands, and the parts are re-machined in Wood Green. There, computer-controlled lathes make turn parts from solid bars of brass. Nearly everything is hand-polished – a very difficult job, Bigland explains, because you must keep the curves.

The company holds a royal warrant and has been involved with refurbishment projects for the Royal Household.

In 2018 Jeremy Bigland visited the site as a property developer and came away as the company's new co-owner.

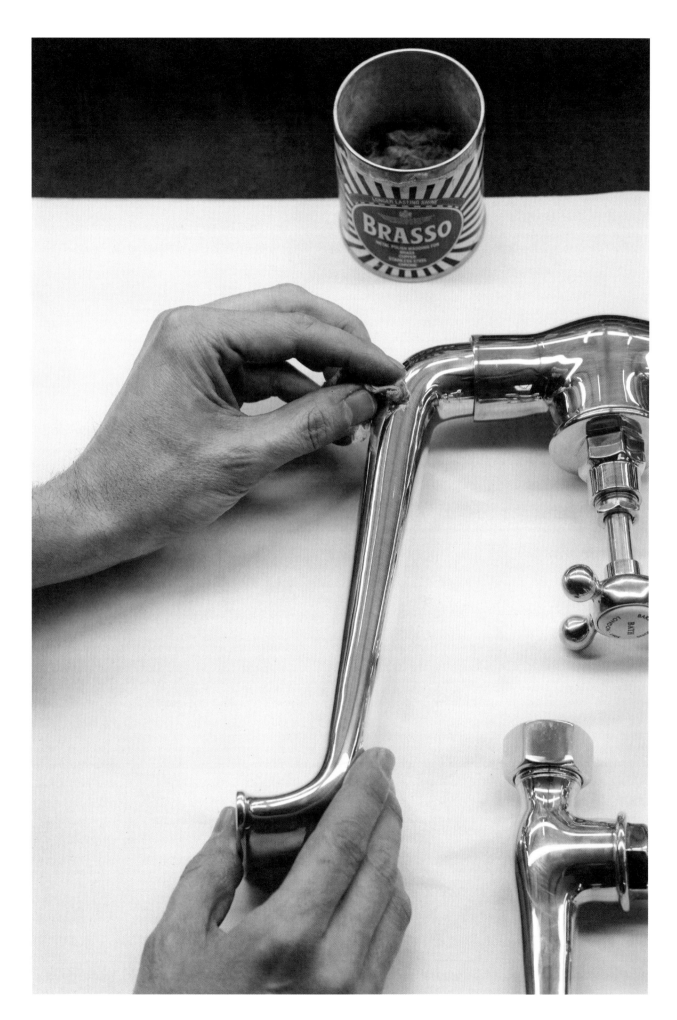

The pulleys in the roof are relics of the shaft-and-belt system that drove the old machines. The sliding covers of the skylights were drawn during the Second World War when bombers flew overhead. Henry Ryan (bottom right) has worked for Barber Wilsons for forty years.

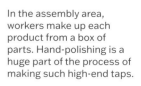
In the assembly area, workers make up each product from a box of parts. Hand-polishing is a huge part of the process of making such high-end taps.

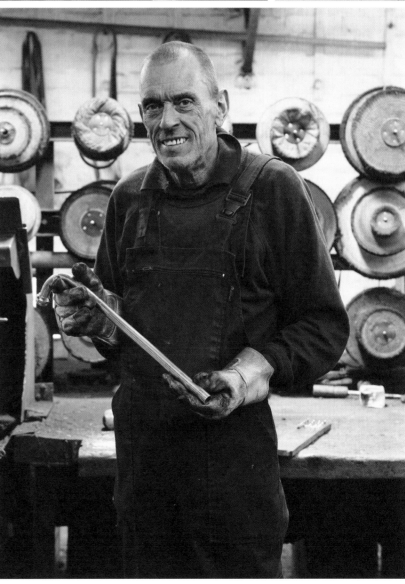

Gary Harrington (right), who joined Barber Wilsons a few years ago, has been a polisher for four decades.

Bellerby & Co.
Globes

Stoke Newington
bellerbyandco.com

The production of each Bellerby globe involves at least five pairs of hands. Once a map has been printed and cut up to sit around a sphere, the key tools are hands, water and glue.

This is quiet work, because one slip can mean that a whole globe is ruined. 'You must concentrate incredibly hard or you'll make a mistake', says founder and map-lover Peter Bellerby. 'You can't have a conversation about what you did last night.'

The business was born out of Bellerby's hunt for an eightieth-birthday present for his father. The globes he found were either 'poor modern replicas or priceless antiques', so in 2008 he set about making one himself. Quite a change from his previous job, setting up and running a bowling alley in Bloomsbury.

Today Bellerby's twenty-five globemakers, painters, woodworkers, metalworkers and cartographers make 600–700 globes a year, in a working mews in Stoke Newington. Bellerby describes the 1950s industrial building as 'very nondescript'. But behind the black double doors is a huge space, where natural light pours through the frosted panes at each end of the pitched roof and is diffused across the first-floor workbenches. Up there, the pieces of map – known as gores – are carefully glued to each perfectly spherical globe. Each sphere is made in-house from resins, Perspex and plaster of Paris sometimes inlaid with hessian fibres, using a mould created by Formula 1 fabricators. The painters then apply layers of watercolour to represent oceans, mountain ranges and vegetation. In terms of the amount of detail, Bellerby explains that 'it's as if you're looking at it from the International Space Station'. Some globes stand on wooden bases turned by fellow Londoners Nichols Bros (pp. 166–69).

The artists work around the sphere in sections one painstaking inch at a time, taking six to eight weeks to paint a big globe. Many globes are bespoke: 'We sell more than half abroad, and a huge percentage of those people come to the studio and see what goes on here before they commission.' So being in London – which is also Bellerby's home city – is an advantage.

Personalized Bellerby & Co. globes are now in the hands of 'heads of state, secretive organizations, Hollywood actors and a geologist, who wanted an Ice Age one', says Bellerby. 'No one else in the world is offering that level of bespoke service.'

Most of the fine work is done upstairs, under the pitched roof. Some staff are trained as globemakers and others as painters.

The founder Peter Bellerby's original plan, hatched in a King's Cross pub, was to make just two globes: one for his father and one for himself.

The painters are taught Bellerby's style and technique. They start with simple washes of colour before learning how to shade a whole globe in detail.

Some customers want their globe to depict their own travels, perhaps showing them on a camel in Egypt. The turned parts of the wooden bases are made by Nichols Bros (see p. 169).

Jost Haas
Glass eyes

Mill Hill

Jost Haas has been making glass eyes for seven decades. At the age of fifteen, he became an apprentice glass-blower, and now, in his mid-eighties, he is the last glass-eye maker, or ocularist, in the UK.

Haas was born and grew up in Germany, which is well known for glass-eye making. Furnaces in the town of Lauscha, in the central state of Thuringia, supply ocularists with the very pure glass that they require.

Haas came to the UK in 1968 to take over a practice from another German ocularist. 'I needed to be in London because clients were used to coming here', he explains. Patients are directed to him by Moorfields Eye Hospital and by accident and emergency units. Before the pandemic, Haas was seeing around five clients a month.

Haas works from his home in Mill Hill. His tiny front room, with its white walls and carpet tiles, is his workspace. A desk is covered with eye-making kit: glass rods and a Bunsen burner.

To make a new eye, Haas cuts off a piece of glass tubing and blows a hollow ball on the end of a rod. He fits an 'iris' disc on to the ball, and combines different-coloured glass to achieve the right colour. Then he adds a pattern of veins to the sclera (the white of the eye). The new eye ends up as a thin hemisphere, which fits over the non-functioning eye, if it is still in place. If not, the hemisphere fits over a ball that has been surgically implanted into the eye socket and attached to the eye muscles.

'The patients sit next to me for up to three hours and leave with an artificial eye in their socket', Haas explains. Glass eyes must be replaced every few years. 'What was nice over all the years, was that people were terribly loyal', says Haas. One such regular visitor was the late actor Leo McKern, who played the barrister Horace Rumpole in the 1980s TV series *Rumpole of the Bailey*.

Now semi-retired, Haas has no one lined up to succeed him: 'I feel it's a little bit too late to have an apprentice.' In the meantime, 'I'll carry on as long as I'm able to.'

Haas's is a dying skill because nowadays people tend to get fitted with plastic eyes, unless they are allergic to that material.

Jost Haas, ocularist, says he is providing a service rather than running a business from his front room in north London.

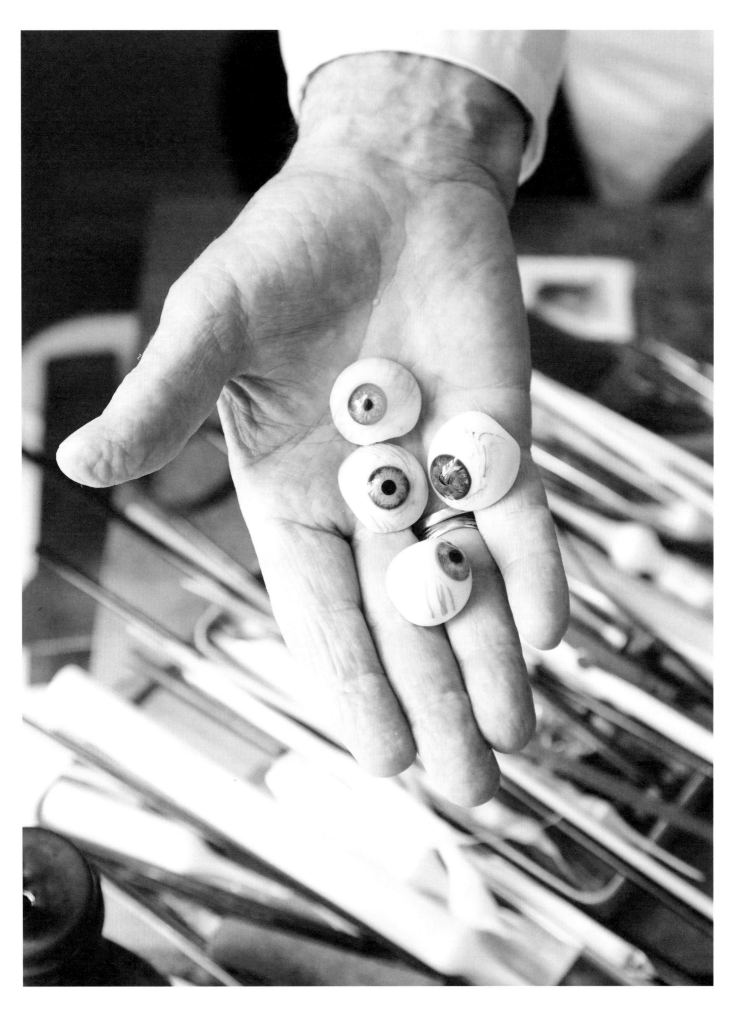

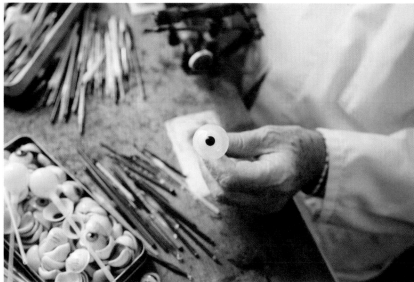

Most prosthetic eyes have some movement, and the biggest challenge for Haas is to get the fit right. Patients leave his front room with their new 'eye' in place.

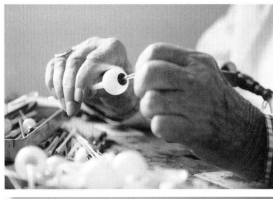

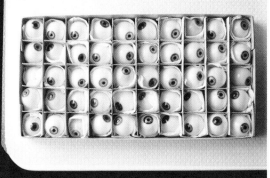

Although he has no apprentice, Haas is happy to share his knowledge, and he welcomes artists, photographers and writers into his work area.

Optical Works London
Spectacle frames

Kensal Green
opticalworks.london

In 2012 Rocco Barker started teaching himself to make spectacle frames from scratch, and two years later he had fashioned a pair good enough to sell. To learn the skill, he picked the brains of the few remaining frame-makers, among them Lawrence Jenkin of the recently defunct London spectacle factory Algha Works.

Barker set up a hotchpotch collection of ageing machinery and a newer cutting machine in the basement of an optician's opposite Trellick Tower, a two-minute walk from his home.

The room is full of acetate frames in various states of completion. There are fifty steps to make each pair, including much precision-cutting, milling and polishing. Barker carries out all this work sporting a pair of his own statement frames. 'It's like a cross between precision engineering and freehand sculpture. You must have a certain dexterity and an artistic flare', he says.

Frame-making is a far cry from Barker's former career as a guitarist in the post-punk band Flesh for Lulu, which toured in the United States for much of the 1980s. There, Barker indulged his passion for vintage spectacles, scouring local flea markets for finds.

When the internet and downloads put a damper on his music career, Barker rented a shop in Portobello Road and started selling off his 2000-strong collection of frames: 'But once they were gone, they were gone, and I thought they can't be that difficult to make.'

Now in his sixties and trading as Optical Works London, Barker makes about ten frames a week. His customers are spectacle brands, including General Eyewear and ByOcular. He also collaborates with fashion designers such as Natasha Zinko and Martine Rose, making frames to their designs or reworking a design from his archive. These frames are stocked in boutiques around the world.

Barker hopes to juggle frame-making with the unexpected revival of his music career. Before Flesh for Lulu, he was in the short-lived band Wasted Youth. The remaining band members have re-formed and are gigging again. But to pull off this dual career, Barker needs to boost his workload and find someone to train up and handle orders when he is on stage.

The basement workshop is strewn with finished and half-completed frames of different-coloured Italian acetate, which is malleable and, according to Barker, holds its shape better than plastic.

An east Londoner by birth, Rocco Barker was a guitarist in rock bands before he reinvented himself in middle age as a maker of spectacle frames.

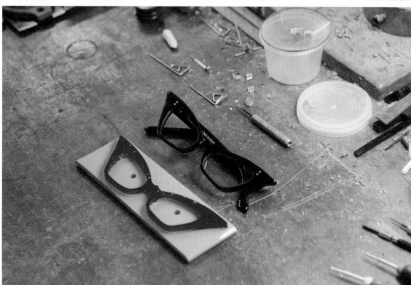

Barker explains that there was a huge eyewear industry in London and Kent until the late 1970s. But by the time he became interested, most of the producers had closed down.

Barker has had to get to grips with fifty processes to make each frame, including heating up the bridge (above, right) and pressing it in the 'bumping machine' to make the raised area.

VEHICLES & PARTS

Brompton
Foldable bicycles

Greenford
brompton.com

Brompton bicycles get their name and *raison d'être* from London. The folding bike was designed and built here in 1975 by the inventor Andrew Ritchie in his flat overlooking the Brompton Oratory in South Kensington. 'He was frustrated by cycling in London', says Brompton CEO Will Butler-Adams. 'If he'd lived in some rural idyll it would never even have come into his brain.'

Brompton moved out of two Chiswick sites because 'we were bursting at the seams', explains Butler-Adams, a mechanical engineer by training who joined the company in 2002. The company's £2.5 million HQ and factory in Greenford is a big grey shed boasting a mezzanine breakout space complete with pool table, ping-pong and piano, and windows looking out over the vast production areas.

On the ground floor, some of the site's 350 staff produce 75,000 bikes a year – including the Brompton Electric – making Brompton the UK's largest bicycle manufacturer. Every bike is hand-brazed by skilled bike builders. Each brazer trains for eighteen months before they are given their 'signature' number and letter code. They stamp this on the parts of the bike that they work on.

More than 70 per cent of those bikes are exported to forty-seven countries. This involves dealing with such 'small challenges' as trade agreements and export duties that change all the time – 'So we must stay ahead', says Butler-Adams. Globally, Brompton employs 750 members of staff.

Efforts are currently being made to increase production capability, develop new products and improve the customer experience. According to Transport for London, between spring 2019 and autumn 2020 the number of cycle journeys increased 7 per cent in inner London and 22 per cent in outer London. 'The future is bright for cycling', Butler-Adams adds.

However, Brompton's success is squeezing it out of London. As Butler-Adams explains, 'Over the past eighteen years, we've seen an annual average growth rate of 17 per cent, and demand for our bikes continues to increase.' That demand, coupled with rapidly increasing rents in London, has forced the company to look beyond the city. The plan is to build a factory near Ashford, Kent, by 2027, when the company expects to employ more than 1500 staff. Meanwhile, its Greenford factory will continue to operate until at least 2030.

A Brompton bike folds up to a third of its size. The standard model weighs around 11 kilograms (24 lb), and the electric version is 16.6 kilograms (37 lb).

Standing in long rows, each wielding a blowtorch in front of a partially built frame, dozens of brazers join the steel parts together by melting copper into the joints.

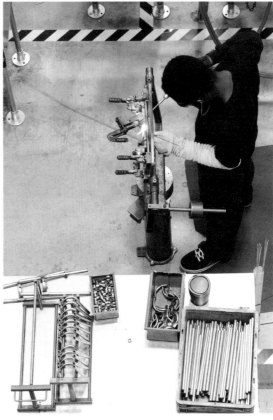

There are fifteen Brompton Junction retail stores in cities around Europe, the United States, Australia and the Far East, and the bikes are stocked in 1500 independent bicycle shops worldwide.

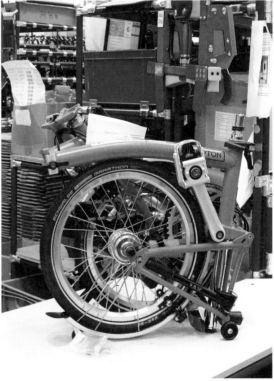

More than 500,000
Bromptons have hit the
roads since the first bike
was made in 1975 by the
inventor Andrew Ritchie.

T. Norris Marine
Boat propellers

Isleworth
shop.tnorrismarine.co.uk

'We're starting to tell customers not to slam the door on the way out in case the building falls down', says manager Simon Norris. The boat-propeller maker has been in the same place – a two-floor, single-skin brick building with a corrugated roof – since Simon's great-grandfather and grandfather set up the business in 1947. 'It's served its purpose', Simon adds. 'It wasn't built to last this long.'

Simon's great-grandfather Timothy was a metal merchant, and Timothy's son Peter was a Second World War pilot. After the war, Peter bought ex-Admiralty marine equipment at auction and sold it on from the property they built. Once Admiralty stock dried up, they moved on to marine engineering and fabricating, catering for Thames pleasure boats. Nowadays, the business makes propellers, propeller shafts and stern gear (bronze castings, machined to order, that attach the propeller to the boat) for commercial and pleasure boats all over the world.

Much of the work entails the replacement of old, tired stern gear. 'We've got regular customers who've been coming in for seventy years, and now their grandsons are coming in', Simon says. While other companies mass-produce items, 'we can copy things by hand exactly'.

Simon, who has a background in the marine industry and a keen interest in boats, has been involved in the business since 2015. His uncle Jonathan Norris, who is managing director, has been with the company since the mid-1970s and now works from home. When Jonathan started, there were six people working at six lathes. Today the building is too big, because it is just Simon and long-standing employee Steve Cheshire on the shop floor; the foreman, Brian Perry, retired in 2021 after fifty-one years. Simon says he is proud that his family's firm has managed to employ people for such a long time: 'It's nice to think they've had a job for life.'

As the shareholders struggle to agree on the company's future, T. Norris's fate is uncertain. The floor is thick with bronze shavings, but there is no time to sweep up: 'We're still trying to churn out enough stuff to survive with hardly any employees', Simon explains. Even with these staffing levels, the business makes several hundred propellers and shafts a year.

Manager Simon Norris, great-grandson of the co-founder Timothy Norris, has been with the business since 2015. The company has been in the same premises for more than seventy years.

The propellers are cast in manganese bronze elsewhere and then polished in-house. T. Norris Marine bores the tapered hollow in the middle of a propeller on a lathe. The bore must be accurate, so that the propeller fits on to the shaft.

Long-standing employee Steve Cheshire works on the shop floor with Simon. The company's oldest machine is around ninety years old.

To change the angle of a blade, the root of the blade is heated and then gently twisted. 'Not many people are able to do that', says Simon Norris.

BIZ Karts
Go-karts

Brimsdown
bizkarts.com

In a purpose-built factory in Enfield's Brimsdown – the second-biggest industrial estate in London – more than 1200 go-karts are produced a year. From the chassis to the graphics, they are custom-built to order by BIZ Karts' twenty welders, fabricators and assembly staff.

The family-run set-up started in Shoreditch in 1816 as a builders' merchant called Smith & Sons. In the early 1900s a metalwork division was added to supply products such as zinc guttering. During the Second World War, the firm made aircraft drop tanks (auxiliary fuel tanks carried on the outside of planes). After the war, it became BIZ (standing for Builders Iron & Zinc Work) and now comprises two companies: thirty-strong BIZ Engineering and forty-strong BIZ Karts.

BIZ Karts was founded in 1994 when Mike Smith, managing director of BIZ Group,

met some leading figures in the UK karting industry. 'Mike was looking for a niche product we could manufacture and sell', says his son Chris Smith, who is a director of BIZ Karts. 'Go-karts seemed a good fit, as he had a keen interest in motor sport, having raced motorcycles in the early 1980s.'

Some BIZ Karts staff have been with the company since the beginning, but, as Chris explains, 'sales are outgrowing what we can produce, and it's difficult to find people with assembly skills'. So the firm is considering apprenticeships. This growth is in part due to exports. A sales office opened in Florida in 2017, and now roughly 40 per cent of all karts are exported to the Americas. 'We have more people working in the business than ever before,' says Chris, 'so managing the space efficiently can be a bit tricky, with no room for external expansion.'

This 4180-square-metre (45,000 sq. ft) factory, which sits opposite the Warburtons bakery, is being refurbished. Inside, it is split into four sections. The twenty or more welding bays service BIZ Karts and BIZ Engineering; the laser-cutting and CNC punching machines cut raw sheets of metal to make parts such as pedal sides and bracketry; in the assembly section, everything is built on to a painted chassis; and the warehouse holds components and parts, 70–80 per cent of which are made in-house.

There is an increasing appetite for BIZ's electric kart. It attracts a different customer base, and with karting tracks opening in defunct shopping centres, more families are getting involved.

There are no other go-kart manufacturers in the capital, says Chris Smith, and only a handful in the UK. 'But none of the others is making our type of product to our scale.'

Chris Smith, who is a director of BIZ Karts, is the son of the founder. But the company's roots go back to an early nineteenth-century builders' merchant.

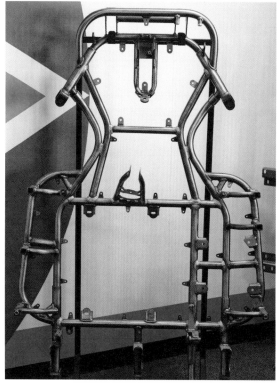

Each chassis is fully hand-welded and straightened in the factory. The chassis is painted and the kart's components are added in the assembly section.

'Some kart manufacturers sell to individuals for racing, and their karts are as light as possible', says Chris Smith. 'Ours are built for the demanding rental-kart market, so must be strong and durable.'

JETMS Completions
Aircraft interiors

Biggin Hill
jetmscompletions.aero

The Covid pandemic hit many companies in the aviation sector, but not all. JETMS Completions' work making cabin interiors for commercial aircraft has been replaced by demand from people wealthy enough to switch from a first-class seat in a commercial plane to a £6 million–£8.5 million private jet.

The company also converts executive jets into private air ambulances 'for people with very good travel insurance', says head of sales, Andrew Tarry. And as commercial airlines adapted to taking cargo on their main decks during the pandemic, JETMS built smoke barriers to protect the flight decks.

These developments mean that staff numbers have been stable at forty-four. The thirty production workers, some of whom have been with the company for fifteen years, are based in a 2800-square-metre (30,000 sq. ft) hangar. There, the wood workshop produces bespoke pieces such as galleys, bars and tables, which are lacquered and varnished in spray booths. As well as working on new planes, the team fully refurbishes twelve aircraft a year.

The company was founded as RAS Completions at Biggin Hill Airport in 1996 by two local businessmen with a background in aircraft painting and cabin construction. The airport was formerly a Royal Air Force station famous as a fighter base during the Battle of Britain in the Second World War, and is the home of the Spitfire. So the company also repaints and refurbishes these heritage aircraft in the Biggin Hill Heritage Hangar.

Avia Solutions Group, a privately owned Lithuanian firm with several aviation businesses around the world, bought the company as its London base in 2021. With Avia's investment, the plan is to renovate the Biggin Hill facilities and to construct a second hangar. JETMS Completions already

has a base at Stansted Airport. The aim is to have the same at Luton and Farnborough and possibly Gatwick. And from Biggin Hill, which is 30 kilometres (19 miles) south of central London, the company intends to service Continental Europe and then the Middle East. 'London is a meeting point for everyone', says Tarry. 'It's a hub for international trade and is hyper-connected.'

Tarry adds that these ambitions will involve upskilling and increasing the workforce, taking on more apprentices and bringing in more machinery.

Andrew Tarry joined as head of sales in early 2021. The company is looking to increase its workforce as it expands beyond London Biggin Hill Airport.

The Biggin Hill Heritage Hangar houses the world's largest collection of Spitfires and a 1940 Hawker Hurricane. Tours are offered of its Spitfire restoration facility.

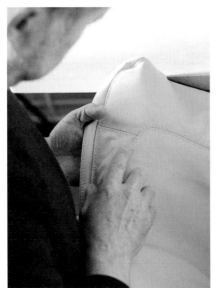

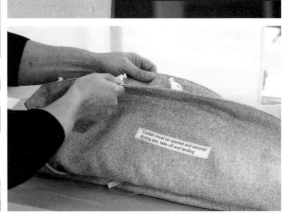

The workshop specializes
in interior repairs and
manufacturing and exterior
paint refinishing, as well as the
creation of new interior and
exterior paint schemes for
VIP and commercial aircraft.

A jet receives a total overhaul: the old paint is stripped with chemicals and the body primed for new paintwork.

Richmond Bridge Boathouses
Wooden boats

Richmond upon Thames
richmondbridgeboathouses.co.uk

Richmond waterfront had its boatbuilding heyday from the 1860s until after the Second World War, according to master boatbuilder Mark Edwards: 'Big businesses were building thousands of rowing boats for hire.' But with the arrival of river launches and other forms of entertainment such as TV, and the extension of pub opening hours, 'boating dwindled'.

These days, Edwards, who has an MBE for services to boatbuilding, is the driving force behind the Thames boatbuilding industry. Operating out of four underground stone vaults dating back to 1777, he makes around four boats a year and restores between seventy and eighty.

In front of the arches is a large, vibrant promenade with buskers, and there are slipways and steps for accessing the water, as Edwards also hires out boats. 'It's rather an eighteenth-century scene', he says.

His grandfather and great-grandfather had been shipwrights in Penzance and St Ives, and in his youth in the early 1970s, Edwards worked at Richmond on boat hire and occasional repairs. In 1980 he set up as a boatbuilder in Hampton, and in 1992 moved into the Richmond workshop. There, a number of boatbuilders traded as individuals. And as the others retired, Edwards expanded his business into adjacent vacated boathouses. The closest boatbuilder on the Thames is at Chertsey, he says.

Edwards makes vessels mostly for boat clubs and private customers. 'We earn most of our income from filming', he says – that is, either providing boats from which action can be shot, or building boats for sets, such as for Ridley Scott's film *Robin Hood*: 'We're always doing something unusual and interesting.' In 2012 Edwards and his team worked on the build of the 27-metre-long (89 ft) Royal Barge *Gloriana*, which was presented to the Queen on her Diamond Jubilee.

Richmond waterfront is 'one big family of largely self-employed individuals with boating at the heart of it'. So when Edwards secures a big contract, there are plenty of craftspeople to add to his two long-standing staff. However, he adds: 'People would love to turn everything into coffee houses. It threatens our rent and use of the arches.' And if that happened, 'it would be a sterile waterfront'. But Edwards and his peers have dug their heels in: 'It's hopefully got quite a good future, not just for me, but also for other boat hire and boat clubs.'

Luan Qeloposhi (opposite, bottom), originally from Albania, first gained work experience with Richmond Bridge Boathouses when he was sixteen and still at school. He now works for the company full-time, and his brother Gazmir is also employed there.

Master boatbuilder Mark Edwards, MBE, comes from a family of Cornish shipwrights and is determined to keep boatbuilding going at Richmond Bridge.

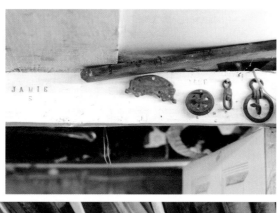

Bill Robinson (top right) helps
Mark Edwards make and
repair wooden craft, including
racing skiffs, pleasure and
racing punts, electric canoes,
small launches, sailing boats
and lesser-known whiffs and
shallops. Edwards has even
made a wherry.

At high tide, Edwards is able to float boats from the arches out to the river. There are also slipways and steps for accessing the water.

ELECTRICAL
FITTINGS & GLASS

Electro Signs
Neon signs

Walthamstow
electrosigns.co.uk

Glowing light structures at different stages of production are scattered across the workbenches of Electro Signs. This is where signs for Raymond Revuebar in Soho and for the film sets of *Superman IV* were created.

Welshman Richard Bracey came to London, learnt the neon-sign trade and in 1952 set up his own business. At first, his company made neon advertising signs. When it became popular as artwork for the home, Richard's artist son, Chris Bracey, began treating neon as an artistic medium. He started out by making signs for Soho's strip clubs and brothels. His talents were spotted by Hollywood, and he began fashioning props for such directors as Stanley Kubrick, Tim Burton and Christopher Nolan.

Home is an industrial estate in the heart of Walthamstow Village, surrounded by craft breweries, designers and architects. Among the company's sixteen staff are neon glass benders and fabricators. Chris's son Matthew Bracey explains, 'Neon is quite a scientific product to make. It involves the bending of glass, bombarding the tube to remove impurities, electroding and filling it with one of the noble gases, usually neon or argon.'

Electro Signs makes hundreds of signs every year, many for the booming film industry in London. As well as *Superman*, its pieces have appeared on the sets of *Mission Impossible*, *Lost in Space*, all the Batman films, James Bond … the list goes on.

For Matthew, being in London means 'we're on the high-frequency rail network, so clients can access us easily and we're well placed for deliveries'. And it is easy for Electro Signs' engineers to travel in and out of central London to carry out repairs.

Matthew thought 'the 100-year-old process of making true neon' might be threatened by LED lighting. But that has not happened, and the firm works happily with LED: 'It has its place and benefits, but it doesn't work in competition with neon, which can be repaired and can last for over twenty years without a problem.'

Next to the workshop, the Braceys run God's Own Junkyard, the world's biggest collection for hire of light boxes and signs in neon, bulb and LED. The showroom – an Aladdin's cave of neon signs and ephemera – has been used for photo shoots for titles including *Vogue*, and attracts tourists from all over the world.

Next door to the workshop is God's Own Junkyard, the Braceys' treasure trove of neon signs for hire (also seen on p. 91, bottom).

Matthew Bracey is the grandson of the founder, Richard Bracey, who in the 1950s made and installed the enormous glitzy signs for Soho's cabarets.

Full of signs in production, the workshop is always bursting with colour from the glowing neon and LEDs. The team both creates and installs the signs.

Electro Signs makes and collects eye-catching signs for companies wanting fabulous visual merchandise pieces in their shop windows or in-store.

Jochen Holz
Glass objects

Stratford
jochenholz.com

At Jochen Holz's Steiner school in Germany, his favourite lessons were the various crafts, from basket-weaving to silversmithing. But glass-blowing was not taught. 'I was intrigued', Holz explains, so he spent three years training as a lampworker to make scientific laboratory equipment. However, 'I knew I didn't want to do that as a job; it was to learn the skills.' He came to the UK and studied glass at Edinburgh College of Art and the Royal College of Art.

Holz's individual glass pieces are now in UK galleries, design shops and showrooms, including The New Craftsmen and SCP, and also sell in Continental Europe and the United States.

After college, it made sense for Holz to stay in London because 'I had more connections here than in Germany. Part of going to college is the network you can form.' Plus, he found there were good work opportunities here. He began fabricating for other artists, until he started becoming known for his own work around 2010.

Holz's raw material is tubes made of heat-resistant borosilicate (or Pyrex) glass. The tubes are of different sizes and thicknesses and Holz re-melts them with a bench burner. This technique, which was developed to make scientific instruments, allows him to create more complex shapes, such as his quirky flower vases and oversized neon light sculptures.

Holz likes to push what is possible in terms of size, shape and colour: 'The making part is always important. Through that I'm discovering new things.' He says that his pieces are not pure art, but have a 'light function'.

Holz works alone in his studio in Stratford. It is in a 1970s light-industrial brick unit operated by Acme, a charity that offers affordable artists' studios. His ground-floor space has high ceilings and 'shelves full of glass stuff', as well as many oxygen bottles and glass tubes in boxes, two kilns, a workbench and a tiny kitchenette.

Holz feels he is part of the scene of London designer-makers involved in small-scale production, and has participated in a number of collaborations, notably with the multidisciplinary artist Rose de Borman. But he insists, rather than growing the business, 'I just want to grow my creative practice and make different things and keep exploring.'

Contemporary glass artist Jochen Holz was born and brought up in Germany. In his Stratford workshop, in the shadow of the London Stadium, he specializes in organically shaped lampworked glassware.

Each object is shaped by Holz from flowing forms of hot coloured glass. Pieces include tumblers, wine glasses, vases and sculptural neon lights.

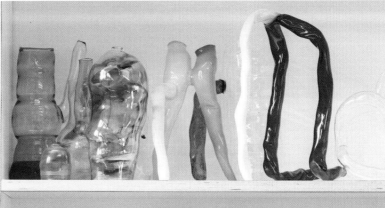

Lampworking is a technique in which glass is heated using torches. Holz prefers to work with borosilicate glass because it is heat-resistant.

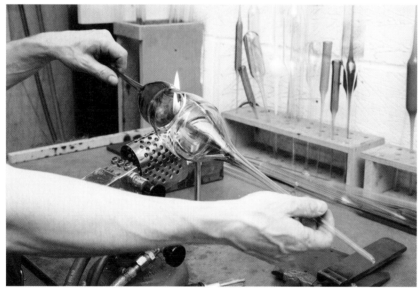

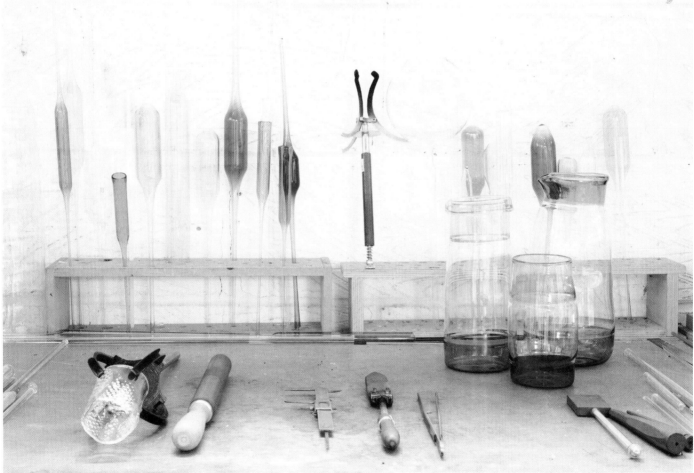

Holz gives texture and shape to some pieces by pressing the molten glass against different surfaces, such as perforated metal or burnt wood.

Cox London
Lighting and furniture

Tottenham
coxlondon.com

Millmead Industrial Estate in the heart of Tottenham is home to food businesses, music studios, joinery and car-repair workshops, a charcoal vendor and places of worship. Husband and wife Chris and Nicola Cox bought a workshop shed there in 2007. Coincidentally, their 1930s double-height brick building was apparently once home to a foundry and metalworks. 'It's got lovely old Sheffield steel beams', says Chris, and the roof, with its north-facing skylights, provides good working light. As the business thrived, the couple leased three more units and now have forty-five staff, of whom thirty are craftspeople.

Cox London designs and makes highly sculptural pieces of lighting and furniture. Every piece is commissioned, and around 90 per cent of production is based on the line of products shown on the company's website. Most commissions come from interior designers furnishing private homes. 'They're hugely important to us, and have these extraordinary budgets', says Chris. They may ask for pieces to be made slightly differently, bigger, in another colour, or wired for the United States.

Cox London has its own foundry on its 1860-square-metre (20,000 sq. ft) site, for investment casting in bronze, and there are hefty forging machines. At the twelve noisy workstations, the architecture of the pieces is hammered, wrought, welded and assembled.

Chris and Nicola met in 1993 on the fine art sculpture course at Wimbledon School of Art (now Wimbledon College of Arts), where they both specialized in metal. After college, they worked for other people, but 'we were always working on the side for friends and family,' says Chris, 'and that personal work took over'. They set up Cox London in 2005. 'Our real success has been starting out as two fine art

Cox London's founders, Chris and Nicola Cox, are trained sculptors. They produce lighting and furniture – much of it with metal elements.

sculptors with £100 between us, and carving out a niche in the world of art that suited our way of working and satisfied and utilized all our creative urges and making skills, and making that niche commercially viable', Chris adds.

There is a great tradition of metalware, silverware, jewellery and glassware in London, says Nicola, who is from New Zealand. 'We're proud to be one in a long line of specialist artisan makers based here.'

The next challenge is to open what Chris describes as an 'eye-wateringly expensive' new gallery on Pimlico Road. It is a massive upgrade from their previous space there, and will allow them to show off their larger items.

There are other foundries in London casting artists' work and making precision parts, but having so many processes under one roof makes the firm unique in their city, the Coxes believe.

The finishing – gilding, lacquer work and patination – happens in the 'clean' workshop. For glass, stone, timber and precious stones, Cox London turns to external workshops, many of which have moved to larger premises out of town.

Standard items, such as mirrors, take twelve weeks to make; other creations can take much longer. 'Our biggest overhead is time, as so much craftsmanship goes into our pieces', says Chris Cox.

Aimer Products
Glass products

Brimsdown
aimer.co.uk / leverint.co.uk

In 2021 Aimer Products branched out. It set up a new business, Leverint, which designs and makes glass lighting. The company was already producing for other lighting companies, but 'we'd always wanted to do it for ourselves', says John Leveridge. So Aimer went into partnership with the lighting designer Andrew Print, and can now make between forty and sixty lighting products a day.

The move has benefited from Brexit: 'Customers want to buy British because of the nightmare of getting stuff from Europe', John explains.

Before Brexit, Aimer had predominantly made between twenty and sixty pieces of petrochemical glassware – products used in the testing of crude oil and aviation fuels around the world – a day. It also made some bespoke hand-blown biomedical glassware for lab research.

The ten-strong company was set up by half-brothers George and Bert Aimer in the early 1900s. Pioneers in the construction of glass X-ray tubes, they operated out of small commercial premises off Tottenham Court Road, near two hospitals. They conducted experiments without realizing that the radiation entering their bodies was causing irreparable damage: George lost his sight and Bert lost several fingers, which were amputated because of radiation burns.

David Leveridge joined as a glass-blower in the mid-1950s and became sole owner in the late 1980s. After his death in 2020 aged eighty-three, his son and daughter took over. John had started at Aimer straight from school, doing acid etchings on laboratory glassware, and Lee, who is in charge of administration and accounts, joined in 1995.

Aimer was based in Camden Town for thirty-five years, until it moved to Enfield in the mid-1990s, to shorten the commute of key staff

living in nearby Chingford. The factory is down a small alley in Brimsdown, one of London's most important industrial areas. It is in a large warehouse that has been divided into smaller units, one of which is occupied by a food-packaging business.

Being on the outskirts of the capital is good for access to central London, where many of Aimer's customers – among them universities, hospitals and architects – are based. The downside, according to John, is the cost of being this close to the centre.

There used to be more glass-blowers in London, when universities had their own glass-blowing departments. Even so, the city's small glass-blowing scene is reasonably vibrant. As for Aimer, the plan is to bring in a handful more people to work on Leverint. 'Lighting is going to be one of our main focuses, moving forward', says John.

Siblings John Leveridge and Lee Rowland run the company, which was established by half-brothers George and Bert Aimer to make glass X-ray tubes.

Aimer's new venture, Leverint, is a partnership with lighting designer Andrew Print (left) to design and produce its own range of lighting.

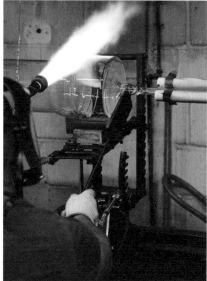
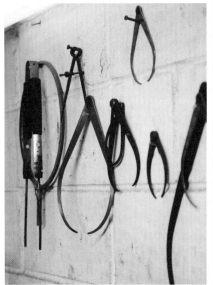

Much of Aimer's glass is hand-blown on the bench. 'The most skilful part is the glass-blowing', says John Leveridge. 'It takes years to learn.'

In the factory, there are huge gas canisters and burners to heat and mould glass. Intricate measurement lines are etched on to biomedical test tubes and jugs.

Supertuff
Toughened glass

Park Royal
supertuff.co.uk

Karsan Hirani and Devji Meghani arrived in the UK from India in the early 1980s. To begin with, they worked in the building and glazing industries. Together, they set up Supertuff in Park Royal in 1999.

Although there were already toughened- and processed-glass manufacturers in the area, 'they thought there was space for another company', says Ritesh Hirani, son of Karsan. 'They called around local companies and built up a customer base, and quite a few are still customers today.'

Now with 130 employees, Supertuff is the UK's biggest independent supplier of toughened glass, and has a fleet of twenty-five branded lorries. Operating twenty-four hours a day, five days a week, it processes approximately 250 orders per month. Order quantities vary greatly from a few panels up to 200 pieces.

Some of the eighty staff on the factory floor have been with the company since the beginning. They are all issued with hard hats, safety glasses and thick gauntlets. There is a lot of automated machinery, including cranes with suckers that attach to the glass and carry it from one process to the next. Such automation minimizes handling of the glass and thereby reduces the risk of staff injury and of glass becoming scratched or chipped.

Suppliers deliver glass in its untreated form to Supertuff's 9300-square-metre (100,000 sq. ft) premises, its third home in Park Royal. Different machines cut the glass to size and shape, polish it and do cut-outs (for plug sockets, cat flaps and such like) and arris (to smoothen sharp edges).

'Our specialism is processing – that is, creating cut-outs and polishing – thicker plate glass, which requires more sophisticated machinery and trained operators. That's the most skilled element', Ritesh explains.

Ritesh Hirani is the son of co-founder Karsan Hirani, and has been a director at Supertuff since 2019.

The glass is toughened in one of the three on-site toughening furnaces, which can reach 200°C.

Much of the cut, arrised and toughened glass goes to double-glazing companies. Glass fitters use the processed glass for balustrades, balconies and flooring. It is also used for office partitions, and more recently high-street restaurants have ordered Covid screens.

Park Royal gives the team good access to suppliers and customers, many of whom come to the factory for collection.

The ground floor comprises the factory, where much of the machinery is automated, while the mezzanine houses offices and storage.

The new furnace (bottom), bought in 2021, saves on electricity bills and allows for a quicker turnaround time for the important process of glass-toughening.

Supertuff has supplied special glass for Tottenham Hotspur's new stadium, Heathrow Airport and Harrods, and more recently has made Covid screens for restaurants.

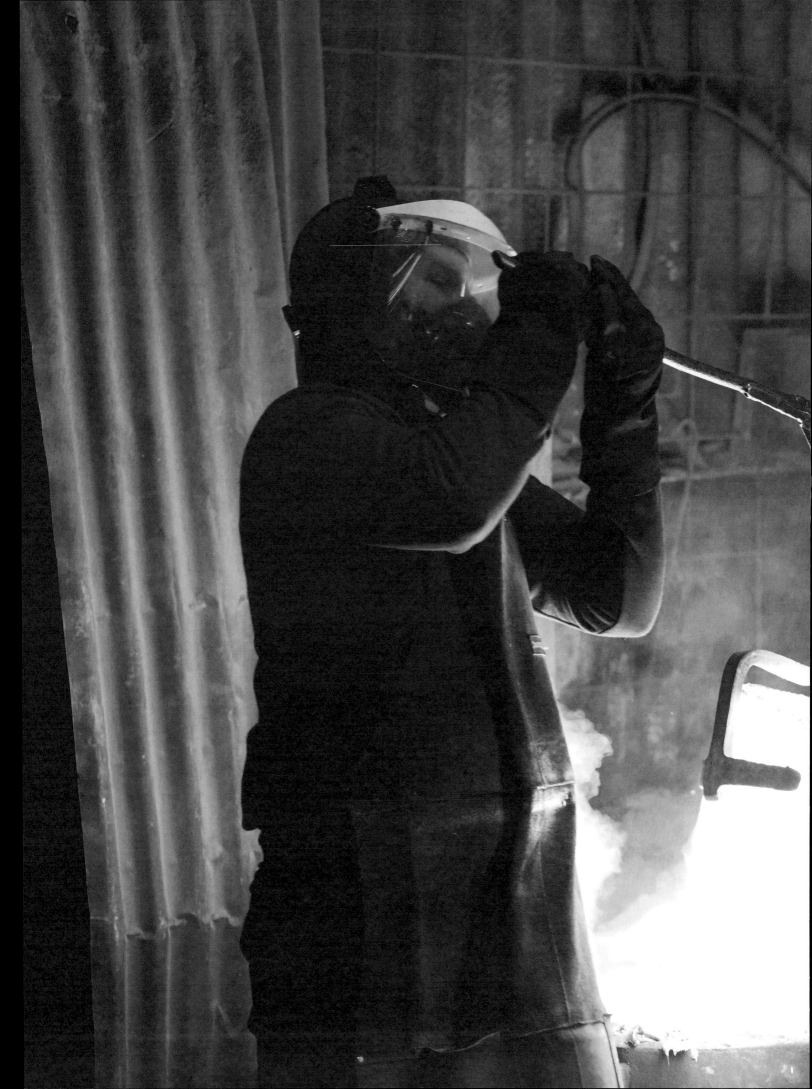

METALWORK

Kaymet
Aluminium trays

Peckham
kaymet.co.uk

Without the help of computer-controlled machines, Kaymet produces close to 25,000 aluminium trays a year. It also makes electric table hotplates and trolleys. These items go into shops, hotels, restaurants and even yachts and aircraft in forty countries.

In its 1960s heyday, when the hostess trolley was a must for dinner parties, Kaymet employed nearly 200 people. But tastes changed, and by 2013 sales supported only three employees. The business anticipated closure before a just-in-time rescue by Mark Brearley (co-author of this book) with his wife and brother. 'There's something very appealing about a business that's survived for a long time because it has a good, well-made product', says Brearley. 'We thought that we could reposition, spruce up the way the business comes across and give it more visibility.' Since then, Kaymet has more than tripled its production, is back up to fourteen staff, exports 70 per cent of output, and has been granted a royal warrant.

Kaymet was established in Elephant & Castle in 1947 by Sydney Schreiber, who previously worked out of the basement of his family's radio shop nearby. 'Once, London was a major centre of metal-based engineering businesses', says Brearley. Now it is less so, but the remaining cluster would still be the envy of most cities, and it includes the UK's only aluminium tray and trolley manufacturer, and 'as far as we know, one of only a handful in the world'.

Kaymet is now based in a 1950s former printing works, off the Old Kent Road. Visitors immediately notice the sound and smell of the old, specialized machinery: the big guillotine slices up sheet metal; the chop saw cuts tubes and extrusions; power presses crop, notch and form; holes and logos are punched in; polishing lathes, grainers and belt linishers trundle and whirr.

Kaymet carries on in the capital 'because we the owners are here, as are our key people', Brearley explains. There is also a cachet to London: 'We have a consumer product, and part of why people like it is that it's made in London. It's a cooler provenance location than England or the UK.'

Despite the firm's longevity, 'national, regional and local government want rid of Kaymet and its like, to replace us with housing', Brearley adds. 'It's our city too, but we're made to feel unwelcome.'

Determined to resist the pressure to flee London, the owners are figuring out how to increase capacity in their existing factory. Meanwhile, Brearley is musing product variants such as tables with wheels, as he works to make the city's manufacturing economy visible.

Kaymet director Mark Brearley is working to secure the future of the business in its part of London and to increase production to meet burgeoning demand.

The production team
are mostly local people.
They are part of a long-
established cluster of
metalworking businesses
in this part of the city.

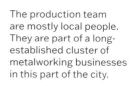

Products leave the factory
with a folded card (above)
that introduces the company
and proudly displays the
classic Kaymet logo, the
royal arms and, on the back,
the Queen's Awards for
Enterprise logo.

Kaymet turns hand-assembly to its advantage by offering a large range of size and finish options. It makes the parts then assembles variants to order.

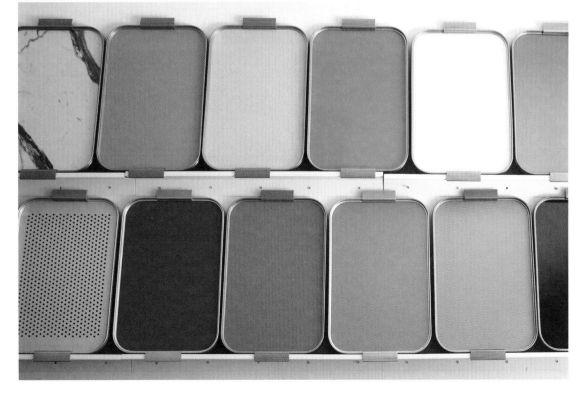

Whitton Castings
Foundry

Woolwich
whittoncastings.com

In the dirt, heat and noise of Whitton Castings, molten metal has been transformed into pieces as varied as a vast hand sculpture for Ringo Starr and railway switches.

When Steve Whitton left school at the age of fifteen with no qualifications, his father suggested that he work in a foundry. 'I took to it straight away', he says. 'At the end of the day, you can see what you've made.'

Whitton set up shop in 1987, and 'even to this day, I still enjoy it', he says. Unusually for a London-based foundry, he casts a range of metals: bronze, brass, aluminium, lead and iron. The foundry is surrounded by workshops in a part of the former Woolwich Dockyard that used to be a hive of industrial activity, with the famous Stone Foundries once a stone's throw away. 'I'm here because I live in London, and I also get passing trade', Whitton explains.

Those are the upsides. The downside is that 'nobody wants a foundry on their road', and the council plans to demolish his building and develop the surrounding site into hundreds of flats. 'I don't know what will happen then,' says Whitton, who is in his late sixties, 'but it would be a great business for someone to take on.'

Inside, two piles of sand are blackened from the casting process. To make a mould, clay and water are added to the sand. 'Whatever shape you've got, you copy it in sand', explains Whitton. 'When you cast up, all the sand becomes hard and hot, and the moisture is burnt out of it. It's amazing.'

'You put the pot in the furnace, you put the solid metal in the pot, close the lid and light the furnace', Whitton continues. He heats the furnace to different temperatures for different metals, from 250°C for lead to 1200°C for iron. Once molten, the metal is allowed to cool – for between thirty minutes and three

Owner Steve Whitton got into casting straight after leaving school. The foundry is dark, hot and noisy. Years of casting up have left the 185-square-metre (2000 sq. ft) space full of samples.

hours – so it can be poured into moulds to set. Whitton then knocks the sand off the casting and grinds the edges smooth with a linishing machine.

As well as Starr's hand, one-off projects have included the New Edinburgh Gate, Hyde Park, and portcullis gates for a building in Davies Street, Mayfair. Both were designs of the late jewellery designer Wendy Ramshaw and came to Whitton via The Sculpture Factory, which engineered both sets of bronze gates. Other one-offs come courtesy of undergraduates: 'I get a lot of students coming in off the street with the weird and wonderful things they've created.' However, it is big-volume, bread-and-butter work – such as twenty brass switches a week for Network Rail (four pieces for each switch) – that has kept Whitton busy.

Most of the orders are big production runs – for example, for the railways – while others are one-off artistic or sculptural pieces.

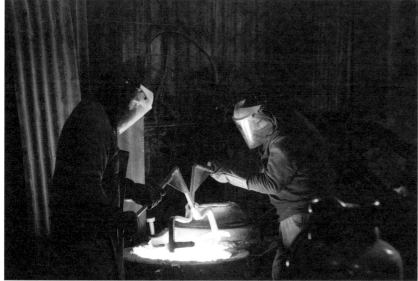

Steve Whitton and his one employee, Nathan Gardner, are able to work in a number of metals, which makes them unusual for a London foundry.

Ormiston Wire
Wire ropes

Isleworth
ormiston-wire.co.uk

Fashionable folk in the late eighteenth century sported corsets and wigs. In 1793 the Scotsman James Ormiston set up shop in the capital to supply spring-wire for these fancy items (rubber was yet to be invented).

Since then, Ormiston Wire has spread its wings, becoming adept at adapting to the times. Half its work was for the defence industry until the Cold War ended in 1991 and 'defence spending was substantially cut, as it was all love and peace then', says managing director Mark Ormiston. The company helped to develop the Charnley saw, a handheld wire saw used in myriad hip replacements, but that was replaced by mechanical saws. And the firm supplied the braid that picked up electricity from the Scalextric car track until the late 1980s. 'Then they moved production to the Far East, and that market disappeared for us', Ormiston adds.

Ormiston Wire is not alone in weathering these storms. In 1971 the UK boasted twenty-nine wire-rope manufacturers. Just three remain, the other two – Bridon-Bekaert and Brunton Shaw UK – making big ropes for ships. 'The other wire companies have gone because they specialized in one type of wire', says Ormiston. 'We've specialized in everything', from the puppet wires for the 1960s children's TV series *Thunderbirds* to lanyards and gym cables.

It all happens behind the large roller-shuttered door of a 930-square-metre (10,000 sq. ft) modern building of brick and corrugated iron in Isleworth, a seven-minute cycle ride from Ormiston's home. Inside, some of the specialized machinery dates from the 1950s. The basic raw material – steel or platinum wire – is twisted, cut and plastic-coated to create wire ropes, strands and braids. 'We're shipping out tonnes of stuff a week', says Ormiston. 'We export worldwide.'

Managing director Mark Ormiston is descended from the founder, James Ormiston, who started the business in the late eighteenth century.

While some industry is being squeezed out of the area, ten-strong Ormiston Wire is secure because the company owns its own factory and other property. But as 'manufacturing sites are being purchased and developed for housing, this causes problems as we then don't have a pool of experienced factory workers', Ormiston explains.

Ormiston's aspirations for the future are family-focused. 'I'm getting on a bit, but when I eventually drop dead, I've got some fellow directors, a good working team', he says. 'Hopefully we'll carry on in the family for a seventh generation.'

Ormiston Wire has had to change with the times, diversifying from delicate surgical sutures to special-effects applications for the film industry and strands for low-voltage lighting.

The wires are often used for one-off projects, such as for the designer Thomas Heatherwick's suspended sculpture *Bleigiessen* in the atrium of the Wellcome Trust headquarters, for Harry Potter's broomstick and for antennas for the British Antarctic Survey in Antarctica.

Mark Ormiston has a keen interest in the environment and energy efficiency, and has installed a wind turbine and solar panels on the factory building.

Grant Macdonald London
Goldsmithing and silversmithing

Borough
grantmacdonald.com

In 2019 Grant Macdonald London moved from a characterful but grubby Victorian warehouse in Clerkenwell, which had been home since 1971, to a glazed twenty-first-century building in Southwark. 'We export over 90 per cent, so for visiting customers we need a beautiful light, airy building because we're making beautiful things', says Grant Macdonald.

Some customers are Middle Eastern royalty. That means 'traipsing through the thick carpets of beautiful palaces' as Grant and his son George, who is managing director, drum up business. These commissions include bespoke *objets*, clocks, trophies and ceremonial swords.

While the company struggles with the capital's high costs, Grant acknowledges the draw of their London address and the city's world-renowned reputation for its gold- and silversmithing and hallmarking. 'It opens doors. It's a huge advantage for us, as people abroad perceive us as being at the centre of everything', he says. Also, there is a network of artisans nearby to call on for such skills as cutting, enamelling and embossing.

As a schoolboy, Grant was practical rather than academic. In 1961 his father, who was a doctor, suggested that he visit the silver workshop of one of his patients. On Grant's first visit, he made a spoon, 'and I thought, Wow! I went back every Saturday. I was bitten by the bug.'

With eighteen staff, Grant reckons this is one of the biggest silversmithing workshops in London. 'They're skilled and experienced craftspeople – four have worked for us for more than twenty years, one for more than thirty years – and we must keep them because there isn't a pool of employees out there to recruit from', says George. The Macdonalds also grow their own talent by training people.

Founder and creative director Grant Macdonald works with his son George, who joined the business in 2003 and became managing director in 2017.

In the sparkling workspace, these craftspeople mix new technology and tradition. From a concept, a prototype is 3D-printed and shown to the customer. A model of the whole item is 3D-printed in wax, or models of separate elements are printed in the same way, and then cast in sterling silver or gold. If there are separate elements, these are welded, soldered or bolted together to create the final piece. 'Then we polish or gold-plate or lacquer the piece', explains George. One of those ceremonial swords takes 250 hours. While they cannot quantify the volume, Grant says they make hundreds of different-sized pieces a year.

Grant recalls tough times, when he had to sell all his wife's jewellery in Camden Market, along with his car, to pay off tax bills. But for now, 'business is good and the future is bright, so long as we're willing to go and get the work'.

Craftspeople combine traditional methods and modern technology to make one-off commissions and small runs of highly prized objects.

The company manufactures many pieces for export, including small animal figurines and ceremonial swords made in gold or silver, which are given as state gifts.

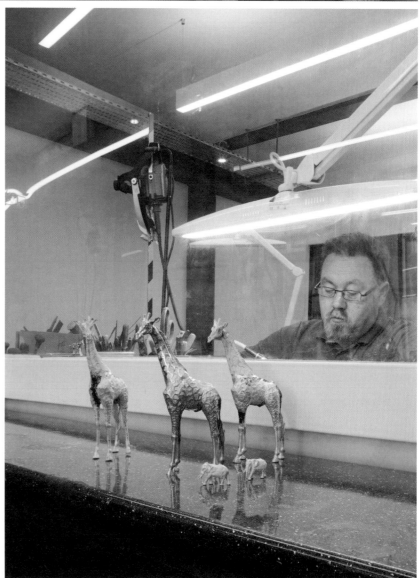

In 2015 Grant Macdonald London was granted a royal warrant as goldsmith and silversmith to HRH The Prince of Wales.

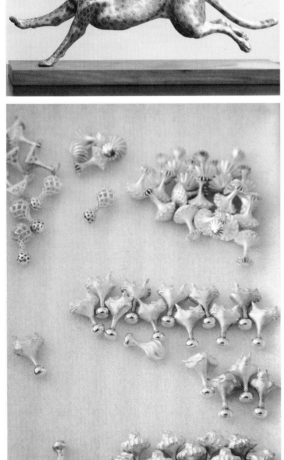

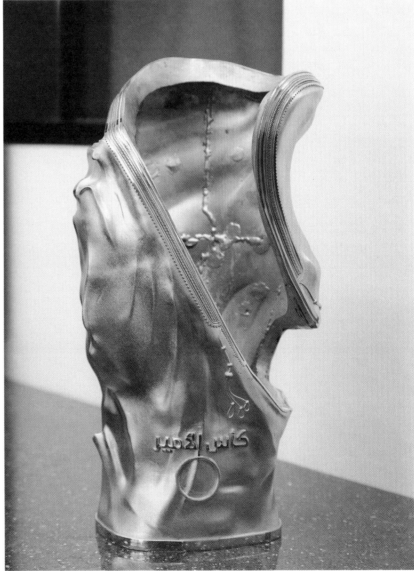

William Say & Co.
Tin cans

Bermondsey
wsay.co.uk

In the office above the factory floor, sales and marketing director Stu Wilkinson (left) has amassed some archival material, including the tea-chest bungs invented by the late William Say (opposite, bottom).

In a still partly industrial side street near the Old Kent Road, cans for Fortnum & Mason's Turkish delight and Farrow & Ball paint are rolling off the production line. William Say & Co.'s brick factory stands on 1.2 hectares (3 acres), a vast site for inner London. Inside, a high-speed Soudronic welding machine turns sheets of tin-plated steel into cylinders, which are then fitted with bases and a variety of lids.

William Say has fifty shop-floor staff. Some have been with the firm for more than thirty years, and one couple has worked there for half a century. Together, they produce eight million items a year. The cans are filled with anything from cakes to paint, polish and aircraft fuel.

William Say – a dapper fellow with a bowler hat, round spectacles and ornate moustache – set up the business in 1930. A serial inventor, his breakthrough had been a humble bung, patented in 1916. When tea clippers docked in London, the only way to sample the product was to prise open the sealed wooden chests. Say's solution was to cut a small hole in the side of a chest. The tea leaves could be scooped out and the hole resealed with his specially designed metal bung.

Four generations of Wilkinsons have been involved with the William Say business, and it is now in the hands of Peter and his sons Garth and Stu. When Peter joined in 1966, inner London boasted forty-seven canmakers. Since then, all bar one have gone out of business or have consolidated and moved out of town. William Say is still here in part because the firm owns its site. Moreover, the fact that it is in the capital means that some customers can easily visit the factory to discuss their particular requirements and watch their order passing along the conveyor belts.

Things started to go downhill for the sector in the 1970s, or as Peter puts it, 'The tin-can industry has been buggered by plastic.' But now the Wilkinsons see that the tide is turning. Consumers and hence retailers are falling out of love with plastic. This is tin-plated steel's chance, they believe, to reclaim its crown.

Today William Say stamps the bases of its tins with messaging about being made in London using the site's solar power, and being 100 per cent recyclable – a classy alternative, in the Wilkinsons' view, to the sorry saga of plastics. What's more, as Stu points out, recent supply-chain problems in the Far East (owing to the pandemic and shipping containers being in the wrong place) 'have accelerated the general trend for buying local. There's a growing thirst for knowledge about how stuff is made, and it adds some value for customers.' The factory buys its sheet metal from Tata Steel in South Wales.

William Say has paired up with Fujifilm in the UK to develop a digital printing press and inks that can be printed on to a sheet of metal. 'On one sheet of tin plate you can have different designs next to each other, and you can control the colours independently', Stu explains. An example is William Say's colourful new sample pots for Farrow & Ball Curated by Liberty, which feature different Liberty textile designs: 'Now we can do any bespoke print – that could be a logo or full photography. And because we're able to do shorter runs, this will develop into a big thing for us.'

The workers produce millions of cans and lids a year, for customers who then fill them with food, paint, aircraft fuel and more.

As consumers increasingly turn their backs on plastic, the Wilkinson family expects packaging made from tin-plated steel, which is recyclable, to come into its own.

ARTS &
ENTERTAINMENT

Royal Opera House
Costumes and props

Covent Garden
roh.org.uk

For anyone who is not on the staff, the Royal Opera House's 10,500-square-metre (113,020 sq. ft) warren of workshops is hard to get one's head around. In the 43,900-square-metre (472,500 sq. ft) Covent Garden building of 1858 by E.M. Barry, together with its 1990s Dixon Jones-designed additions, seventy-eight production staff make props, theatrical models, footwear, wigs, costumes, hats, jewellery, weaponry and more. Scenery construction and painting take place in the ROH's production facility in Thurrock, Essex.

These specialist artisans work on average on 290 opera and ballet performances across thirty productions a year. The director of technical and production, Mark Dakin, who joined in 2015 from the National Theatre, is responsible for delivering all the productions to the stage: 'We've got a deadline every night; the show must go on. The logistics are incredibly complex.' The building, too, is complex, with lifts to different wings and floors colour-coded to help with navigation. Architecture firm Stanton Williams was responsible for the Royal Opera House's most recent transformation, completed in 2018, with the result that visitors can now see into some of the workshops through internal windows.

Antony Barnett, senior production props manager, joined in 1985. He is in charge of a main props workshop area, metal and carpentry workshops, a fibreglass room (where props are carved, moulded and cast), a walk-in spray booth, a dye workshop, a sewing room and an office for sourcing and buying. His twelve-strong team has been tasked with making or sourcing everything from a little Fabergé scent bottle to a 7-metre-tall (23 ft) flaming horse head, rocks, flowers and full-size trees. 'The furniture on stage has to be strong enough to withstand people

Some of the Royal Opera House's myriad workshops in the 1850s Covent Garden building are on view to visitors.

dancing on it and with it', he says. 'The workshop is full of the vast range of materials we use, and in every corner there are lots of things that may make potential props. We never throw anything away!'

This sentiment is echoed by the hats and jewellery manager, Janet Steiner: 'We try to recycle as much as possible.' She has worked at Covent Garden for thirty-eight years, and of her three-strong team, no one has been there less than fifteen years.

Like Barnett and Steiner, many staff have worked at the Royal Opera House for a long time. Dakin says that staff tend to stay 'because they're working with the best directors and designers in the world, on one of the top three opera stages in the world, I think. And in the centre of one of the greatest capitals.'

Propmakers aspire to become as proficient as possible in many disciplines, even down to more niche skills such as bookbinding, flower arranging and calligraphy.

Specialist areas include the dye workshop, where costumes are dyed in large vats, sometimes to match the skin tones of specific performers.

With so many performances going on stage, often with vast casts, propmakers have daily deadlines to either make or repair items.

The Posticherie
Hairpieces, wigs and wig cages

Stoke Newington
theposticherie.com

Catriona Lim had always liked the idea of wigs. She specialized in headwear during her costume design degree, and as part of a project made a wig out of fabric and wool. After graduating, she worked doing wardrobe for West End theatres and was put in charge of wigs. 'I wanted to learn properly', she says, so she enrolled at The Wig Academy in Eastbourne.

After that, Lim phoned wigmaking firms (most of which are based in either London or Bristol) and got a job with the Alex Rouse Wig Company in Tottenham. There, she worked on *Game of Thrones*, *Outlander*, the Harry Potter film series and various Marvel movies, creating hairpieces for the actors, stunt doubles and stand-ins.

The increasing number of high-definition films – which have higher image resolution – has led to good-looking hair becoming more important. 'Things on screen are so scrutinized. You don't want the audience to know that a wig is being worn', says Lim.

Lim set up The Posticherie (*postiche* is French for 'hairpiece') as a one-woman band in 2013 to experiment and collaborate within hair design. She has since honed her skills to specialize in woven hairpieces and wig cages.

Lim mostly uses human hair, and for the front hairline combines it with mohair, which is so fine that it resembles baby hairs. Coarse, wiry yak hair is also used: 'You can get a good frizz with it, so it's ideal for fake beards and moustaches.'

Lim's workshop in Stoke Newington is close enough to London's theatreland and the cluster of film-makers to make it easy to meet clients for fittings. It is in Shelford Place, which comprises three converted warehouses opposite Clissold Park that together accommodate sixty-four businesses, including picture-framers and fashion designers.

Catriona Lim, founder of The Posticherie, experimented with wigs as part of her degree in costume design, and went on to obtain work in the West End.

In her small space, Lim's wigs on blocks sit on shelves, and on the mezzanine are vintage overlocking and sewing machines, at which Lim finishes the wefts (woven lengths of hair). She sorts hair from hair merchants and UK-based salons into different lengths by drawing it through big brushes, and then washes and dyes it at the sink.

Lim's next step is to build up stock to start a hire database: 'Just as you hire a hat for a wedding, you could hire a hairpiece.'

In Lim's small studio, there is room on the mezzanine for her sewing and overlocking machines, at which she works on the wefts of hair.

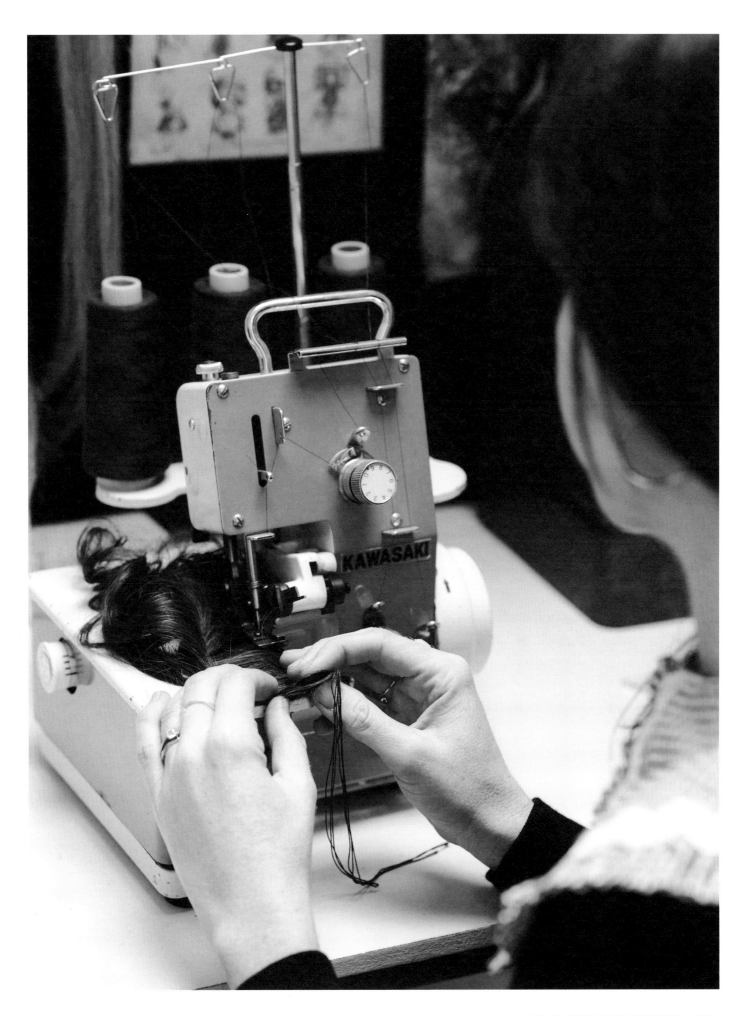

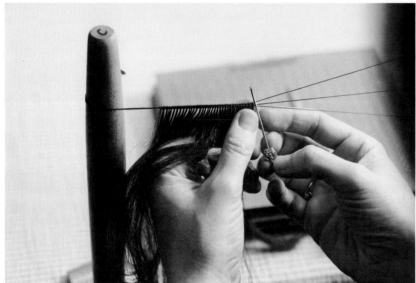

Lim makes wig cages by bending wire into sculptural shapes, and then dresses the wig on top, à la Marie Antoinette.

Several of Lim's wig cages were worn in the finale of the West End and touring production of the stage musical *Hairspray*. And due for release in 2022 is the spy film *Stay Behind*, in which the protagonist, Antonella, wears a wig by The Posticherie.

Marcus Hall Props
Theatrical props

Lewisham
marcushallprops.com

Around thirty years ago, props for theatre productions were mainly handled by stage management. But the nature of shows has changed, says Chris Marcus: 'They've become more extravagant, bigger, more fantastical.' As a result, many props for musicals are now built especially for the shows, 'because they're slightly less real, or very stylized', Jonathan Hall explains. At the same time, set designers are busy people and are often working on multiple projects. 'We're an extension of the designer in a lot of ways', Hall adds.

The two, who met working in stage management for *The Lion King*, set up Marcus Hall Props to fill this gap. Since 2007 they have made props for many of London's most popular musicals, including *Mary Poppins*, *Charlie and the Chocolate Factory* and *Frozen*. And when these big-brand shows tour or open in overseas cities, their props give the productions consistency.

Having started out in a mews in Camberwell, in 2017 the company moved to a bigger space in Lewisham. The studio is surrounded by retail and shares an entrance with a pet shop. Many other scenery people have moved out of town because their workshops have been converted into flats, says Hall.

The metal-framed brick warehouse is stuffed full of props, most of which the firm makes, some of which it buys in. Shelves are stacked high with old moulds, materials and paints, and there are six workbenches. 'Everyone's doing something different every day', Marcus says of the ten freelancers typically on site. 'It's a very varied mixture of good, fun projects.'

From Lewisham, the team are able to reach the city centre quickly, which is useful because they often have at least twelve shows running in the West End. They can do repairs during the day and return them in time for the evening show.

When theatres were closed during the pandemic, the company was forced to diversify, and found new work in retail, display and TV, including creating mannequins of Amy Winehouse for the exhibition *Amy: Beyond the Stage* at the Design Museum.

The aim is to continue to make for other sectors because, as Hall says, the pandemic showed that 'we can't rely on theatre'.

Chris Marcus (seated) and Jonathan Hall say theirs is one of London's biggest facilities creating props for commercial theatre. Their props are found on many West End stages and beyond.

Mannequins of Amy Winehouse were created in the studio for the exhibition *Amy: Beyond the Stage*, which ran at the Design Museum in Kensington from November 2021 until April 2022.

The duo's team of freelancers includes mouldmakers, sewers, painters and carpenters. They outsource upholstery and metalwork. The mezzanine is used as an office and storage space.

Many items are moulded and cast in resin, some in the new rotocasting machine. The use of resin prevents, for example, a wine bottle smashing during a song-and-dance number.

When prams used in the musical *Mary Poppins* break on tour, they are returned to Marcus Hall for repair (left). The company also sources authentic American props via eBay.

Avolites
Live performance equipment

Park Royal
avolites.com

In 1991 Avolites underwent a management buyout led by three employees, including the present chairman, Richard Salzedo (left).

The live events industry is growing and becoming technically more complicated. Bands make a bigger proportion of their income from performing, so more shows tour globally. At the same time, there is an audience that wants to be part of the show but not at it, so joins in online. There are also virtual shows, with avatars. 'These all present opportunities but also complexity for us', says Andrew McKinlay, marketing director at Avolites.

It is a far cry from the company's roots. As McKinlay explains, when Ian Walley was a roadie for rock bands in the 1970s, lighting control and power distribution equipment (aka dimmers) was so fragile that 'he found nothing survived the journey to venues. He was permanently resoldering and repairing.' Walley monitored the electricity supply at venues with his trusty Model 8 AVOmeter (AVO standing for Amps, Volts and Ohms), earning him the nickname Avo.

Armed with a Bachelor of Science degree in mechanical engineering, Walley set out to design and manufacture a better lighting rig. He set up Avolites in his own warehouse in a railway arch in Stamford Brook, Hammersmith, in 1976. His lighting control system was soon in demand worldwide.

In 1985 Avolites moved to its current base in Park Royal, which is home to many companies in the production and delivery of live events, and close to clients, including the BBC. 'A lot of companies from the UK dominate this sector', says chairman Richard Salzedo.

Avolites was bought by a media company in the late 1980s, but the relationship was short-lived, and it returned to private ownership in 1991 after a management buyout led by three employees, Salzedo, Steve Warren and Meena Varatharajan.

Nowadays, Avolites' showstopping piece of equipment is the Diamond 9, a console

that integrates video control and lighting control, operated by one person. Salzedo predicts that in the future 'we'll see those moving lights projecting video images'.

As the buyout directors retire while retaining ownership, a new management team is taking over. McKinlay describes fifty-four-strong Avolites as a relatively small manufacturer, assembling by hand twenty different products – 500 smaller items and ten big consoles a month. 'The point is to grow that', he says, but such manufacturing cannot be done at scale in London 'and still be competitive on price'. So high-volume equipment will be assembled elsewhere in the UK, and smaller-volume, top-end products – such as the Diamond 9 console, which has 10,000 parts – will continue to be made in Park Royal.

Avolites is convinced of its important role. 'We all know we're not saving lives,' Warren says, 'but there's no replacement for shared human experience.'

Many of the production staff are highly skilled software and hardware engineers who have typically worked in other industries such as aviation and automotive. The Avolites Diamond 9 console (opposite, top) was launched in 2021. The Rolacue 30 (opposite, bottom) was first introduced in 1984. The '30' denotes the number of faders on the console.

Many staff come from eastern European countries, where 'they have very good technology universities and manufacturing bases', says Andrew McKinlay, marketing director. Andrzej (Andy) Zurawski (below, left) heads the dimmer production team.

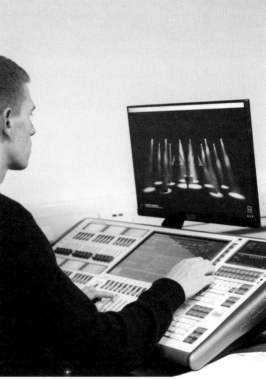

Avolites' equipment has been used at major live events around the world, among them Queen's Magic Tour in the mid-1980s, Glastonbury, the Eurovision Song Contest and the opening ceremony of the London Olympic Games in 2012.

Vinyl Factory Manufacturing
Vinyl records

Hayes
thevinylfactory.com

In its heyday in the 1950s and '60s, EMI's 60-hectare (150-acre) site in Hayes had 20,000 workers, many of them making records. However, the company thought the writing was on the wall for vinyl. When it closed its manufacturing plant in 2001, all the equipment was bought by Mark Wadhwa and Tim Robinson of The Vinyl Factory, which owns Vinyl Factory Manufacturing. These two saw a future for vinyl, and they have been proved right. Every pressing plant around the world is at capacity.

In 2021 Vinyl Factory Manufacturing was set to make 1.5 million records. 'We can't keep up with demand', says manufacturing director Adam Teskey, who has been part of the music industry all his working life.

The company's thirty-two-strong workforce is based in one of EMI's old buildings, Enterprise House. It is the UK's biggest vinyl manufacturer and the only one in London. The records are pressed on EMI's seven so-called 1400 presses, which were custom-built in-house in the 1960s and '70s, so they require much TLC from the engineers. Some staff are ex-EMI, while newer recruits have been trained up. This combination of unique machinery and skilled workforce means that the factory can make 6500 records a day. But demand is such that they do overtime every day and every weekend.

Transport links in Hayes are good for exporting and for reaching customers in central London. And now the local train station is also served by the new Elizabeth line.

Teskey is now watching where the market goes: 'The music industry has had many peaks and troughs, and a lot of people are jumping on the vinyl bandwagon. But we're not in it to stack them high and sell them cheap. We're in it to make the world's best records.'

Manufacturing director Adam Teskey oversees operations in EMI's old building, where the original machinery that pressed records for The Beatles, Pink Floyd and the Sex Pistols is still in use.

Making a record is like alchemy, and involves pungent chemicals and vats of bubbling green liquid. Matrix operators load the electroplating baths, where the metalwork is 'grown' on the silvered surfaces of lacquer discs (far left), and prepare to trim a newly plated disc (below).

A vinyl record is form-moulded out of polyvinyl chloride (PVC) at around 140°C under 100 tonnes of hydraulic pressure.

As the vinyl revival continues, Vinyl Factory Manufacturing is dealing in ever-bigger numbers. Its labels make a colourful display in floor-to-ceiling racks (centre right). The labels are baked to extract moisture before they go on to the pressing machine.

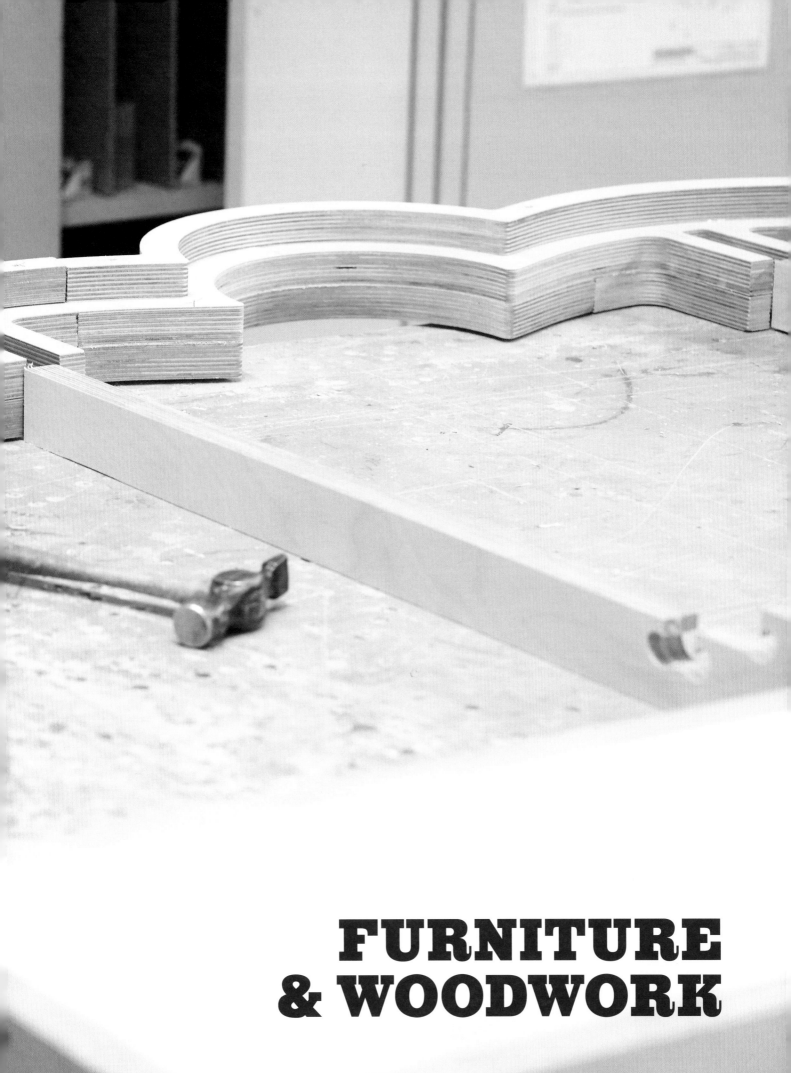

FURNITURE
& WOODWORK

Gavin Coyle Studio
Furniture

Walthamstow
gavincoyle.co.uk

'Old-timers come in and ask for water melons', says Gavin Coyle, because they remember when his building was used to store them. Built in the 1950s as a car mechanic's workshop, it later housed exotic fruit. In 2012 Coyle took over the whole yard, with buildings on three sides, and now he lets out space to a journalist, a psychologist, a set designer and an illustrator: 'It's a little community, and it helps to pay the rent.' Coyle and his two staff – formerly an art technician and a set builder – occupy a large space full of natural light.

From the age of four, Coyle was in his father's work shed, 'using all the machines. Even back then, I got a buzz from having an idea and then making it into a 3D object.' He studied furniture design and craftsmanship, and set up his own business in 2007, later taking the plunge with his own space.

London is home to a large number of independent furniture makers, such as Sebastian Cox, Isokon Plus and Goldfinch. Like many of these outfits, Coyle works with interior designers and architects, making bespoke furniture and fitted elements, mostly for residential projects. But he also makes small contemporary craft products, such as the Chirp bird sculpture and Jac side table. These are sold through shops and wholesale, including Heal's and Twentytwentyone, and online through Coyle's 'side hustle', Anden.

The studio does about nine big fit-out projects a year, with smaller jobs filling in the gaps. Whatever the size, 'we want to make heirlooms', says Coyle. 'That's about choosing the right materials, finishes and style. I don't want to make stuff that's going to go in a skip after a few years.'

After his studies at Buckinghamshire Chilterns University College, the big draw for Coyle was London. The studio's location makes it easy to get hold of materials (although prices have risen), and a lot of clients are still London-based, he says. What's more, 'we had lessons on design history, William Morris and the Arts and Crafts movement, which described people enjoying their work. Morris was born in Walthamstow, so it felt like a spiritual home.'

Founder Gavin Coyle's first workspace was in a shed. Then he worked in shared workshops, before he took the plunge and got his own studio.

The studio building sits in a yard next to a railway bridge in Walthamstow, the birthplace of the Arts and Crafts polymath William Morris.

'We try to preserve a traditional method, using hand tools', says Coyle. In the workshop, these tools sit alongside machine tools (opposite). As well as working with architects and making products for shops and wholesale, he sells smaller items, such as the Jac side table (below), through his online presence, Anden.

Savoir Beds
Beds

Willesden
savoirbeds.com

For Alistair Hughes, managing director of Savoir Beds, two good things are happening: 'People are thinking more about sleep and health, and they like to know what goes into the product they're buying; they don't want to sleep on a bunch of chemicals.' The upshot is 'people are investing more in their beds'. This is excellent news for Savoir Beds, whose average price is £20,000 – forty times more than a standard bed. But from the headboard and mattress to the topper, the materials are natural, and much of the process is by hand.

The roots of Savoir Beds go back to The Savoy. The impresario and hotel founder Richard D'Oyly Carte was obsessed with quality. From 1905 the hotel's beds were specially made by the upholstery firm James Edwards in a workshop off Drury Lane. The firm came to be owned by The Savoy; renamed the Savoy Bedworks, it made and repaired beds only for the hotel and others in the Savoy Group.

When the hotel was sold in the late 1990s, it sold off elements such as the laundry and the bed business – whose staff at the time comprised two full-timers and one part-timer. The bed workshop was taken on by Hughes, a management consultant, and his business partner, Stephen Winston, and renamed Savoir Beds. Having worked on a business plan for a private members' club, 'I realized how badly beds were made and sold, often in the least glamorous bit of a department store,' says Hughes, 'but you spend a third of your life in bed.' And he was aware of The Savoy beds' great heritage, with Liza Minnelli liking the one she slept on so much she had it shipped home.

Savoir Beds' sixty-eight craftspeople are equally split across a workshop in Wales (an existing manufacturer bought by Savoir Beds to increase its capacity) and another in Willesden. They make around 650 and 350

The only point in having handmade is if it does a better job than a machine, says Alistair Hughes, managing director of Savoir Beds.

beds a year respectively. The London site is in the former Carlsberg brewery. Inside, there are two lines of production, and each worker has an oak tool board and a bench. Of the Savoy Bedworks staff, Eddie stayed until he retired, and Arjoon, who started in 1986, heads up cutting and training.

Savoir Beds is in London – where it is the only bedmaker of its size – 'because originally that's where our clients were based', explains Hughes. Although the business was built on hotels, and recently supplied Robert De Niro's Greenwich Hotel in New York, today 95 per cent of its beds go to private clients. About half are exported, and Savoir Beds has sixteen showrooms around the world, eight of which are franchised. Hughes expects exports to be the main growth area, and the firm has also started to sell online.

One of the most skilled jobs is hand-teasing the horse tail, which fills the mattresses. It is coiled into millions of tiny curls as a natural spring, and has a cushioning effect.

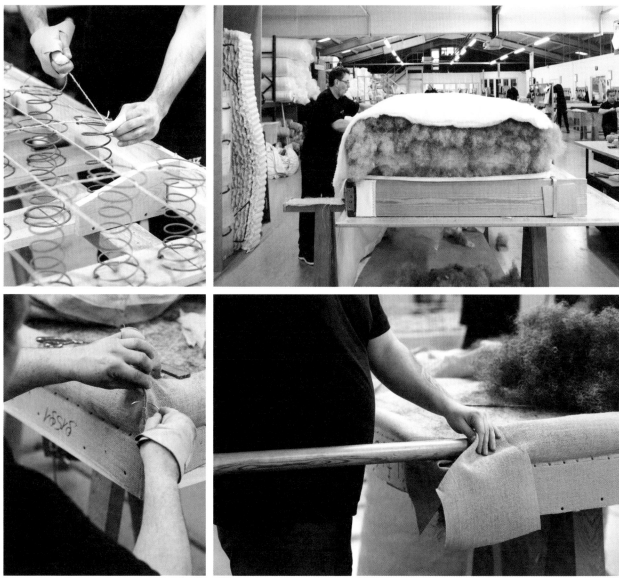

Each craftsperson is responsible for a different part of the bed, such as the mattress, box spring or headboard, and signs each label 'Handmade'.

The Willesden workshop makes the brand's most deluxe beds, called No. 1 and No. 2, which take around 120 hours and 80 hours to complete, respectively. The workshop also makes bespoke elements.

Hitch Mylius
Upholstered furniture

Ponders End
hitchmylius.co.uk

Hitch Mylius's first base in Ongar was good for recruitment. 'From north-east London down towards the city centre there's a corridor of rag trade and curtain-making', says owner Robin Phillips. 'We took on people who'd worked in smaller places, as they had easily transferable skills.'

The company was founded in 1971 by husband-and-wife designers Tristram and Hazel Mylius. They were frustrated by what they saw as a lack of modern design in British-made furniture, compared with output from Italy and Scandinavia. Their first design – the HM11 seating system, which is still sold today as HM18 – was a success in Liberty in the early 1970s. That and other pieces were then stocked by the Conran Shop.

In 1995 the burgeoning company moved to its current premises in a little industrial pocket along Alma Road, not far to the west of Enfield's huge Brimsdown industrial area. Its neighbours include a company making fireproof doors and another that does car repairs. Its business is London-centric and since 2018 it has had a showroom in the contract-furniture hub of Clerkenwell. The Enfield base allows quick and easy access into town.

While there are other upholstered-furniture makers in the capital, most are producing for the residential market. 'Our big competitors are in the north of England and the Midlands', says Phillips. His furniture goes mostly into offices, healthcare settings and transport hubs, and in 2007 it graced the new Eurostar terminal at St Pancras International.

Alma House – a run-down 1950s factory building where metal parts and propellers for ocean-going liners were made – was transformed for Hitch Mylius by architects the Pike Practice.

Of Hitch Mylius's thirty-four staff, around twenty-five are in production. The production manager, Chris, has worked for the company for almost forty years, and several others have been there thirty years. They make 5000–6000 pieces a year, from footstools to corner sofas.

Phillips joined in 2007 from the Conran Shop, and was made director in 2010. He took over the company ten years later, when the founders stepped down. 'I was excited and could see its potential', he says, citing new products planned – 40 per cent through collaborations with external designers – and a new sales team. 'I could see a path forward.'

Once fabric and leather arrive, they are quality-checked. Each piece is then cut by hand, and starts its journey.

A tired factory building was transformed into Hitch Mylius's two-storey production base, with a small showroom and office on the first floor.

Around three quarters of
the production staff have
been with Hitch Mylius
for more than a decade,
several of them for thirty
years or more.

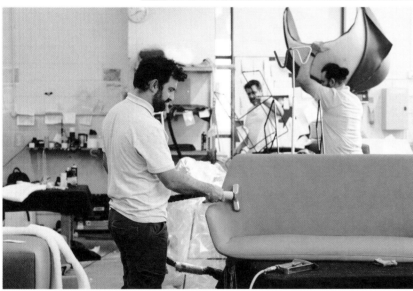

Covers are tailored and sewn with attention to detail, to obtain the perfect fit over the foam. Robin Phillips (above) became owner of the company when the founders stepped down in 2020.

Nichols Bros
Woodturning

Walthamstow
nichols-brothers.co.uk

On a residential street in Walthamstow, behind the grass-green door of an old brick building, hundreds of wooden stair parts are made every day.

Inside, the stone floor is thick with sawdust, wood chips fly from the machinery and the walls are adorned with spindles. Nichols Bros' workshop has changed little since it opened in 1949. 'It's very old-fashioned', says co-owner Geoff Nichols.

The company's roots go back to the 1920s, when five brothers set up Nichols and Nichols in Hackney to service the East End's furniture trade. In 1949 two of the brothers, Stanley and Arthur, established Nichols Brothers (Woodturners) Ltd in Walthamstow. Around 90 per cent of the firm's work is still in the London area, says Stanley's son Geoff, who joined at the age of fifteen. He runs the company – now called Nichols Bros (Wood Turners) Ltd – with his childhood friend Harry Morrow.

In the 1950s Nichols Bros' bread and butter was the ubiquitous standard-lamp base, a stalwart of front rooms across the UK. But since the 1960s the growth in home ownership – and hence refurbishment – has led to the focus being on new and replacement balustrading for stairs.

Nowadays, loft conversions are big business, with builders commissioning the firm to make bespoke parts of the new staircase in the style of the stairs below.

Every bespoke piece starts life on a woodturning hand lathe. 'I turn a sample, we put the sample in the woodturning machine, and the machine copies it', Geoff explains. The workshop makes 100 special spindles a day.

With the firm's specialist machinery, including a 100-year-old wood-twisting machine, Geoff believes, 'we're the last proper woodturners left in London, because we can tackle any woodturning project'. That could be a doorknob or 'an enormous great column for a front door'. Nichols Bros also makes props for film and TV sets and the bases for Bellerby & Co.'s globes (pp. 52–55).

While it still makes sense for the firm to be in London, a big challenge is the local council. 'If they had their way, there would be no parking for any car and everyone would ride a bicycle', says Geoff. That is no good for deliveries and many visiting customers.

If no family member takes on the business, it is likely that Nichols Bros will shut up shop when Geoff and Morrow retire. 'Me and Harry, we're not spring chickens', Geoff points out.

The workshop is very old-fashioned and has not changed much in the last seventy years. Many of the original machines are still in use, and a thick layer of sawdust coats the floor.

Nichols Bros' owners, Geoff Nichols (left) and Harry Morrow, have known each other since they were ten years old.

Nichols Bros makes every component for the construction or replacement of balustrading, from stair spindles and newels to each part of the handrailing. Larger items are turned by hand, while spindles and newels can be made in batches, using copy lathes. The wooden disc (above, right) is a globe base for Bellerby & Co. (see p. 55).

BECK
Interior fit-out and joinery

Chessington
beckinteriors.com

On a large industrial estate in Chessington, a three-storey office building opens out unexpectedly on to a 6320-square-metre (68,000 sq. ft) joinery workshop. Here, bespoke pieces for high-end hotels, museums, residential properties and retail spaces are made.

Joiners sporting BECK logos on their tops craft and assemble the joinery at huge benches positioned down the middle of the workshop. Recent creations are in the Imperial War Museum, Nottingham Castle and the NoMad London and Carlton Tower Jumeirah hotels.

Back in 1995, three carpenters got together to form BECK in Guildford. The business has since been handed down to the board of directors and is currently run by Chris Galloway, Mark Banham and Jonathan Dart. All three have a long history with the company, and Banham began in the workshop on day one.

The production team – joiners, sprayers, machinists, labourers, drivers and seven apprentices – numbers thirty-five and is run by project production director Stephen Middleton, who has been with the firm for sixteen years. Two of the foremen have been there more than twenty-five years, and many others started as apprentices.

'It's unusual for a fit-out company to have a workshop of this size, but it allows us to control the quality of the carpentry', Middleton says. Most of his production methods are traditional, so cabinet doors for bespoke bars and front-of-house desks have mortise-and-tenon joints – a centuries-old joining technique.

In 1999 the firm moved to Chessington because it gave its 7.5-tonne truck and transit van a more direct route along the A3 to deliver materials to its many London clients. Project loads vary, but BECK typically works on a variety of five-star hotels, high-end residential and high-profile museum projects every year.

Middleton is pleased with a new spray booth, which was completed in 2020 and sits underneath the mezzanine. Air-controlled and dust-free, it gives a beautifully smooth and imperfection-free finish to the joinery.

The 300-strong firm, which worked on V&A Dundee, opened BECK Scotland in Edinburgh in 2020, and hopes to add a production facility there in the future.

Bigger pieces are crafted in the workshop, taken apart to be delivered and then reassembled on site. The joiners work with high-quality timber from PEFC-accredited forests.

BECK's project production director, Stephen Middleton, says most of the work comes through tender, and clients are hotel operators, architects, interior designers and structural engineers.

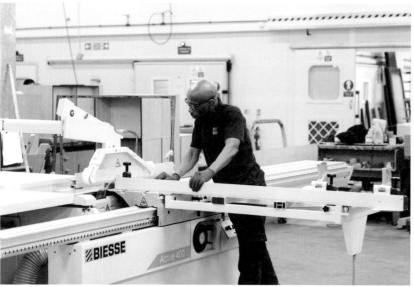

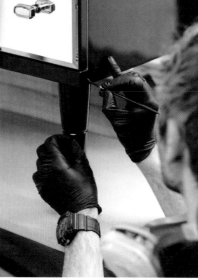

BECK's equipment includes a new spray booth (above), which has resulted in fewer coats of paint being required to achieve a pristine finish.

As well as craftspeople, BECK's team includes operational directors, project managers, draughtsmen, prototypers, planners and finishers.

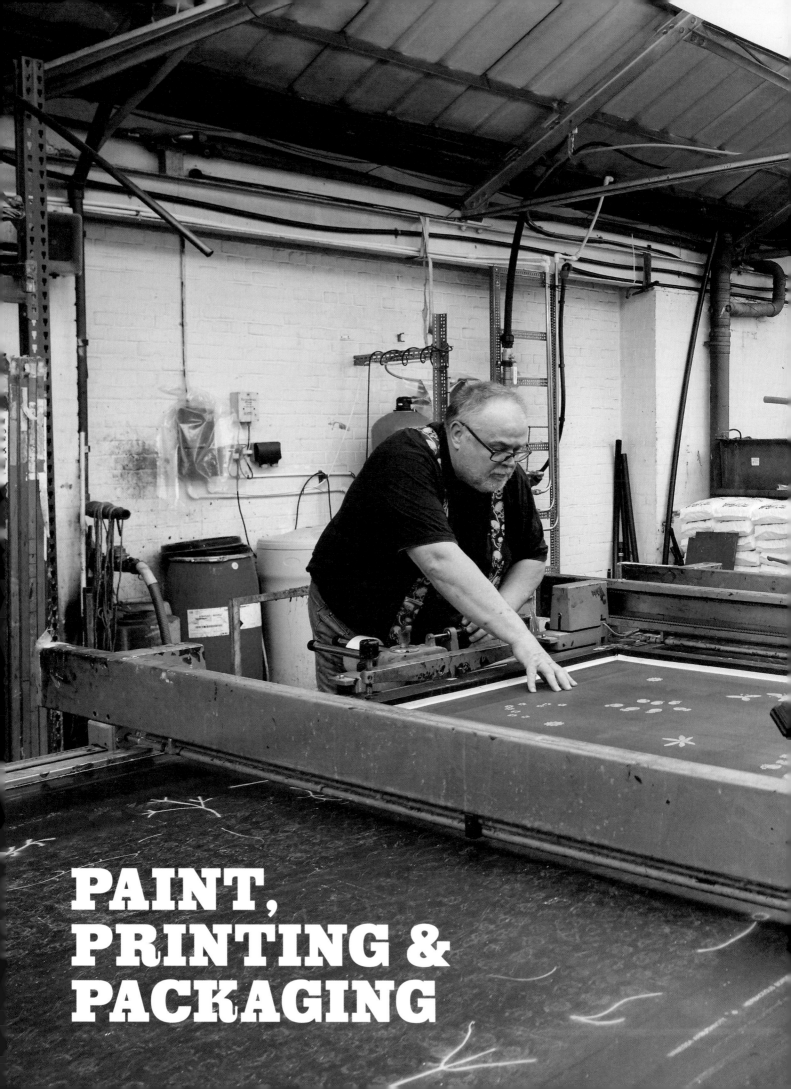

PAINT, PRINTING & PACKAGING

Empress Litho
Printing

Woolwich
empresslitho.com

In the 1980s print was often the mass-communication medium of choice for advertising and design agencies that had products to sell for their clients. These agencies needed technical expertise and speedy delivery, and such requirements led to a boom in colour printing in the capital. Empress Litho was set up by Mick Preston in 1987 in Woolwich Dockyard Industrial Estate to tap into this demand. It built a strong reputation, and its office walls were adorned with awards.

Today the demand for print has been radically reshaped by email and online communications. 'Add Covid into the mix, and it feels as though ten years of change have been compressed into six months', says owner David May, who joined in 1997 and took over on Preston's retirement in 2015.

But the change is not all about decline. May has seen an expansion in demand for luxury and retail packaging as e-commerce has increased. Brexit border troubles also mean that much of what had previously been printed overseas has been reshored. Before the pandemic, less than 5 per cent of Empress's production was packaging. It is now nearer to 30 per cent, and May expects that figure to grow.

Over half of Empress's twenty-four staff members have been with the company for more than fifteen years, and they try to process 2.5 million sheets a month. Lithographic printing uses plates to transfer ink, whereas digital printing typically uses toner powder jetted on to the medium in a press that is rather like a huge office printer. Empress's machinery, including huge Heidelberg lithographic presses and also digital machines, can handle a wide range of projects, from 100 copies of a hardback book to 140,000 copies of an exhibition guide, as well as packaging.

Empress is based in the former Woolwich Dockyard, which was founded by Henry VIII in 1512. The main part of its factory is in the old shell store, a building of beautiful exposed yellow London brick that housed artillery shells for warships. As well as three units in the shell store, Empress has a larger factory in a 1960s building opposite.

As some – perhaps less robust – competitors have gone to the wall, and business confidence returns, things are looking up for Empress. 'The online world makes everything two-dimensional, so if you've got something of value to sell, you need to do it face to face and need something physical, which is print', says May. 'The modern world makes these skills more valuable, sought-after and premium.'

Empress's modern and older machinery, including a foil-blocking machine, delivers high-quality litho printing. Some of the handwork requires dexterity and skill.

David May is the owner of Empress Litho, which handles repro, retouching, proofing and print, through to finishing and binding.

As well as packaging, Empress produces stapled, perfect-bound or sewn soft- and hardback books in all shapes and sizes. Some are for clients who are self-publishing, such as artists.

Woolwich docks used to come up to the factory, and ships would load up with artillery shells, which were stored in Empress Litho's building (far right).

For many years, Empress focused on print materials – such as annual reports and brochures – commissioned through London's graphic design agencies.

Wyvern Bindery
Bookbinding

Hoxton
wyvernbindery.com

'It's a love affair with the craft', says Pauline Leclercq, one of the new owners of Wyvern Bindery. The company was co-founded in 1990 by Mark Winstanley, who studied bookbinding at the London College of Printing (now London College of Communication). When he retired, he passed the business on to his former employees Leclercq (who is French), Julian Pendlebury (South African-British) and Kaori Maki (Japanese).

These three and their handful of part-time staff make exquisite items, including boxes, portfolios and books. 'We're trying to adapt', explains Pendlebury. With the rise of digital photography, the demand for photographers' portfolios has fallen away (the business is down to making about ten a week). And when restaurants were closed during the pandemic, the call for menu holders dried up. But 'home

entertainment is alive and well', Pendlebury adds. 'Film props kept us going and made up 90 per cent of what we were doing.' Hence Wyvern Bindery's props for London's booming film and TV industry. It supplied classroom books for all the Harry Potter films, and Wyvern's is the tome that is cut in half in the fantasy TV series *Game of Thrones*.

Craft bookbinderies are declining in number, and of the dozen or so left in the capital, Wyvern is unusual in that it has a shopfront, so passers-by can see work in progress.

It all happens behind the big shop window of a long, deep unit in Hoxton, to where the bindery moved in 2020 from Clerkenwell. Being in London, the team are surrounded by their customers, from designers and architects to film-production companies and photographers. 'They come in to discuss their projects', says Leclercq.

At the back of the bindery are big, wide workbenches, with shallow drawers holding traditional marble endpapers. Elsewhere are stacked rolls of leather (mostly goatskin), fake suedes (called Suedel), and cloths used for covering hardback books.

Most of the process is by hand. Pages are sewn together, put together with an endpaper and trimmed. Then a piece of board is cut to size to make the cover, and the title is typeset.

Wyvern's team are totally attached to their craft and their most notable product: books. 'I want to keep the tradition of the book going', says Maki. 'The book has a long history. We want to encourage more people to like books.'

Pendlebury echoes this statement: 'It's about keeping the craft alive. Hopefully one or two young people will come and work here, and the craft gets passed on and skills stay alive.'

Wyvern Bindery's new owners, (from left) Kaori Maki, Julian Pendlebury and Pauline Leclercq, are pictured outside their shopfront on Hoxton Street.

As well as making books, boxes, menu holders and photographers' portfolios from scratch, Wyvern carries out intricate repairs on much-loved volumes, such as dictionaries and cookery books.

Wyvern Bindery was responsible for making the book that J.K. Rowling read from during the opening ceremony of the London Olympic Games in 2012.

Julian Pendlebury likens the experience of having a book made to going to a tailor. Drawers and shelves are full of samples of endpapers and cover materials, for customers to choose from.

Mylands
Paints and polishes

West Norwood
mylands.com

The paint for every James Bond film since *Dr. No* has been supplied by Mylands. Set up in 1884, the firm has been working with the film, TV and theatre industries ever since it became involved with British Lion Films in the 1920s.

The paints created especially for these industries are heavily pigmented, often using natural earth pigments. 'That gives the paint a lot of depth', explains owner Dominic Myland. He is the great-grandson of the founder, 'Honest' John Myland, who started as a French polisher at the age of fourteen. After his apprenticeship in Vauxhall, John sold rags and finishes to furniture makers. He then introduced paints, taking particular interest in the art of the colourman. All of John's fourteen children worked in the business.

When Dominic began working at Mylands in the mid-1980s, there were numerous

paint manufacturers in London. Now his company is the only remaining independent manufacturer of decorative paints, he says, as others have been taken over or have sold up, packed up or moved out. Mylands itself had two sites in Brixton compulsorily purchased, so in 1974 it moved to Lambeth's industrial zone in West Norwood, and is determined to stay in London. The firm is housed in four industrial buildings, one of which was formerly a printworks and another a rope factory. There is also a modern warehouse. Of the sixty-five staff, twenty-five are in manufacturing, and some of those have been with the company for many decades.

In 2012 Mylands introduced its Colours of London range and started selling direct to customers and to shops. These days, more than half the annual one million litres produced is this decorative paint. 'The demand for high-quality premium paint is very strong', Dominic notes. From West Norwood, Mylands's fleet of black branded vans can deliver to the company's highest concentration of customers, who are based inside and around the M25.

New shades are created in the old rope factory, where three full-time staff – including a colour scientist – carry out research and development at stainless-steel worktops. The outside of that building (complete with splendid old Crittall windows) is painted in Soho Pink.

Despite the headache of dealing with raw materials shortages, delivery driver difficulties and export red tape, Dominic is looking to introduce new products into the high-end market, to develop new export markets and to keep up with the film industry's requirements.

Some Mylands cans are produced by William Say & Co. (pp. 126–29), a relationship that goes back to the 1930s. Mylands wood polishes account for just under 20 per cent of business.

Dominic Myland is the fourth-generation owner of Mylands, Britain's oldest family-owned and family-run manufacturer of paints and polishes. The company was granted a royal warrant in 1985.

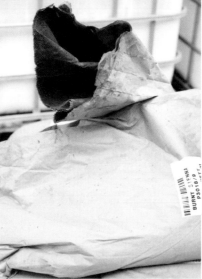

'Making paint is like making a cake mix', says Dominic Myland. Water and pigments combine into a slurry and are mixed into 'dough' by a high-speed blender, and sometimes clays and a china glaze are added.

The challenge that requires the greatest skill is to achieve consistency, to get repeatability. The bestselling paint colour is Threadneedle, a pinkish white.

W. MacCarthy & Sons
Presentation boxes

Woolwich
maccarthyandsons.com

'We put zero effort into going out to get new business', says James MacCarthy. 'Instead, we try to be good to our current customers, and a lot of work comes through recommendation.' With his parents, Michael and Gillian, he runs the family box-making company. Rather than rustling up orders, the three directors 'do everything from talking to customers and accountants to making boxes and doing deliveries', James adds.

Five generations of MacCarthys have been handcrafting custom-made presentation boxes since 1880. Founder William MacCarthy – known as Liam – was born to Irish parents in Peckham, and Irish was his first language. He learnt the trade working with his wife's family business. He then started out on his own from the kitchen table of his Camberwell home.

'A great deal of what we do hasn't changed much', says James, and some of the machinery is almost as old as the business. The corner cutter dates to 1908. The platen, which stamps out the shape of the box, was bought by James's grandfather relatively recently, in 1957.

The factory can offer small runs of up to 1000 units, making it competitive with overseas suppliers. 'It wouldn't be any cheaper to get 250 boxes from abroad, and they'd take longer to arrive', James says, adding, 'I think we've benefited from people wanting to be eco-conscious. We get customers asking about sustainability.'

Including the three family members, there are eight in the factory. One lady, Pat, has worked there for more than thirty years, and Eileen retired in 2020 after thirty-two years. In 1997 the business moved from Bermondsey to the Woolwich industrial estate that is also home to Empress Litho (pp. 176–79). 'The rates were increasing, the business was struggling and we needed to downsize', explains James. 'We've always been in London', he adds, and the location makes it easy for the firm's many local customers to visit.

The premises are a historic dock building with thick brick walls and big arched windows. Inside, as well as those lovely old machines making a clickety-clack sound, piles of finished boxes and materials are strewn about.

Meanwhile, the MacCarthy name is still famous in Ireland. Liam was a huge fan of hurling and in the 1920s commissioned a trophy – the Liam MacCarthy Cup – which is handed every year to the winners of the All-Ireland Senior Hurling Championship.

For presentation boxes known as 'paper over board', the box shape is made and then paper is glued on. Small batches are done by hand, larger orders by machine.

James MacCarthy with his parents, Gillian and Michael. They make two main types of packaging, using different printing techniques, materials and sizes to meet customer requirements.

Wire-stitched boxes are stapled in the corners. Rolex, one of the firm's biggest customers, returns repaired watches from its factory in MacCarthy & Sons' brown stapled boxes.

Most of the preparation and finishing is done manually using hand-operated machines. The oldest piece of machinery was patented in 1894 and made in 1908.

Ivo Prints
Textile and wallpaper printing

Southall
ivo.co.uk

On any weekday, three or four customers travel from around London, and from the United States and elsewhere via nearby Heathrow, to a trading estate in Southall. There, they discuss their ideas and watch their designs being printed. Ivo Prints is unusual in that 'we allow our customers on the shop floor while we're printing', says managing director Michael Haas. 'They find it invaluable to play on the sampling table.'

Michael's mother, Ellen Haas, set up the firm with her cousin Ivo Tonder – like Ellen, a Czech immigrant – in 1963. They were sought out by fashion's elite: Ossie Clark, Celia Birtwell, Zandra Rhodes and Vivienne Westwood. Ellen put designers' work into a commercial form, so that it could be printed successfully.

The company started in a Paddington mews. 'Exciting times,' says Michael, 'but the floor was so rotten, a stiletto heel would go through the floorboards.' As its clients became more successful, Ivo Prints moved west to premises big enough to handle higher volumes. The business has been in its 3440-square-metre (37,000 sq. ft) ground-floor unit since 1985.

In the early days, everything was hand-printed, and staff had to work round the clock to fulfil orders. Even now, hand-printing is the heart of the business. So visitors are greeted by three 53-metre-long (174 ft) manual screen-printing tables. 'I find it soporific watching the screen going down the table, printing', Michael says.

But the bigger space has room for automation: an eight-colour rotary printing machine prints continuous stripes; a flatbed printing machine prints 500 metres (1640 ft) an hour; and two digital printing machines produce wide-width wallpaper. In the colour kitchen, staff mix a tonne of colour a day. Ivo does around 330,000 metres of printing a year, comprising 275,000 metres of textiles and 55,000 metres of wallpaper. Meanwhile, the public can buy fabrics in its mill shop.

With forty-five staff, Ivo is one of the largest textile printers in London. A major customer is the interiors brand Christopher Farr. It has designs in its collection by the highly influential and flamboyant Hungarian-born stylist Michael Szell, who created interiors for Buckingham Palace. On returning from an exotic holiday in the 1980s, Szell said to Ellen, 'I want pomegranates.' She bought one and created a design from it. Called Carnival, it is one of Ivo's most popular designs and is still printed on a weekly basis.

Michael Haas is managing director of Ivo Prints, which specializes in printing furnishing fabrics and wallcoverings for many market leaders and also contract commissions for palaces, embassies, hotels and private residences.

The factory offers such services as screen-making, fabric preparation, finishing and storage, hand and machine screen-printing and digital printing.

David Jolly (right) is responsible for washing down the screens in this booth.

Howard 'Podge' Voyce (bottom left) has worked at Ivo Prints for forty-five years. The fabric at bottom right is Carnival by Christopher Farr, one of the most enduring designs in Ivo's vast archive.

FOOD & DRINK

Hayman's of London
Gin

Balham
haymansgin.com

Miranda Hayman's great-great-grandfather loved experimenting. A pharmacist by trade, James Burrough made insect repellent, cordials and gin. It was the last that proved most successful, and in 1863 he opened a small distillery (known as a gin house) in Chelsea, at a time when gin was hugely popular and London was home to many such premises.

The James Burrough company and its famous Beefeater brand were sold to Whitbread in 1987. Today Beefeater is owned by Pernod Ricard and made at London's largest distillery, in Kennington. However, James's great-grandson master distiller Christopher Hayman felt that his passion remained in distilling. He bought back a small part of the business, including a bottling facility, so that he could continue the family trade.

In the late 1980s, many UK drinkers were drinking vodka, and gin was not on trend. 'So he mostly made small batches of gin for overseas markets such as the USA and Japan', explains Christopher's daughter Miranda, who now runs the fifth-generation business alongside her father and brother James.

Ever since that 1860s Chelsea gin house, the family has been making gin in London, apart from a small break before they moved to their current distillery in a light-industrial area of Balham in 2018. The brick building had at one time been a brewery. 'The location was perfect for transport links, as well as being tall enough to house our gin stills', Miranda says, adding how important it was for the brand's image that the distillery should be back in the capital.

The distillery is home to three copper-pot stills. There is one distiller, who loads the botanicals (a mix of herbs, spices, dried fruits and all-important juniper) into the stills, where they infuse in the English wheat spirit for a full day before distilling takes place on the second day.

These days gin is a very busy category, with a large number of craft distillers across the UK. While there are several other London distillers, fifteen-strong Hayman's is the oldest family-owned gin distiller in England, and its gins have won many awards over the past fifteen years of this gin renaissance.

Around 85 per cent of Hayman's gin is sold to sixty overseas countries. In the UK, around 60 per cent goes to the on-trade and the rest is sold for consumption at home.

Co-owner Miranda Hayman says the company still allows two days to make its gin, while some other distillers have reduced the time.

It is tradition in the distilling industry to give stills women's names. Each one here is named after a female member of the Hayman family: Marjorie, Karin and Miranda.

Flavours are developed in the laboratory. On the mezzanine above is a training bar, where Hayman's hosts cocktail masterclasses and events.

Prestat
Chocolate truffles

Park Royal
prestat.com

Prestat has changed hands four times and is now part of a fourth-generation Italian business. It was founded in 1902 by the Frenchman Antoine Dufour, a master chocolatier who created the chocolate truffle and opened his first shop on South Molton Street in Mayfair. Since 2019, Prestat has been owned by Domori, a subsidiary of Polo del Gusto–Illy Group. Production is based at west London's Park Royal industrial complex – home to around 43,000 workers across 1700 businesses, many of them food manufacturers. Known as 'London's kitchen', it feeds one-third of Londoners on a daily basis, according to Park Royal Business Group.

One big warehouse houses Prestat's factory, where truffles are made and packed, and the office. A second warehouse next door stores the raw material and packaging. The eighty staff are equally split across the two warehouses. Some of them have been with the company for more than twenty years, while the younger members give it 'a start-up feel', says Prestat's CEO, Micaela Illy. There is some automation, but 'there's always a "hand touch", such as hand-rolling or adding decoration'. And even packing truffles is a delicate process, she adds.

The team makes an impressive 100 million chocolates a year – 90 per cent truffles, the rest bars and thins – making Prestat 'the only chocolate factory in London on an industrial, rather than artisanal, scale', according to Illy.

Since Domori bought Prestat, Illy has been looking to invest in more efficient production processes, including updating the IT, and in relaunching the brand to focus on its London heritage.

Illy admits that, with the cost of labour and space, 'we could have a much bigger factory and warehouse outside London'. But retail customers such as Fortnum & Mason, Selfridges and Liberty come to visit, and recently Prestat launched on Deliveroo and the surplus food app Too Good to Go, both of which are focused on servicing Londoners.

Around 30 to 40 per cent of these treats are exported, mainly to Italy. Illy's intention is to take the brand further afield.

Under its new owner, Prestat, which has twice been granted a royal warrant, is embarking on a rebranding and introducing new recipes.

Micaela Illy, who became chief executive in 2022, says Prestat's truffles are made with a 'crazy attention to quality and the best raw materials'.

The ganaches (fillings) are cooked in-house, and a machine fills each chocolate shell via a nozzle. The shells sit in a fridge, then another layer of chocolate is added – a process known as the truffle being 'enrobed' – and finally each truffle is hand-decorated.

As part of its rebranding, Prestat has been reviewing its packaging in an effort to use less material, eliminate plastic and reduce waste.

PRESTAT

LONDON ESTABLISHED 1902
FINEST CHOCOLATE AND TRUFFLES

NET WT. 7.1oz - 200g℮

Tate & Lyle Sugars
Sugar and syrup

Silvertown
tateandlylesugars.com

In buildings and tanks of different shapes, sizes and ages spread across a 20-hectare (50-acre) site, 50 per cent of the sugar sold in UK shops and 80 per cent of the sugar used in restaurant kitchens and canteens is refined.

By the time he was thirty-six years old in 1855, Henry Tate had six grocery shops around Liverpool. Two decades later he bought an old shipyard on the Thames and in 1878 set up a sugar refinery, where the refinery operations are still based.

Meanwhile, the Scot Abram Lyle joined his father's cooperage business and then developed a career in shipping. Like Tate, he moved to London for the size of the market and its status as the centre of global trade.

In the 1880s, Lyle was melting sugar at his 1.2-hectare (3-acre) Plaistow Wharf refinery in Silvertown, just 2.4 kilometres (1½ miles) from Tate's factory. Lyle's Golden Syrup is made by refining the treacle-like by-product in the cane-sugar refining process, which would otherwise go to waste. It was first sold in tins in 1885, and today 100 workers make more than one million units a month.

The rival businesses, which between them refined about half of the UK's sugar, merged in 1921. By the late 1930s, Tate & Lyle was operating the world's biggest cane-sugar refinery, staffed until the 1950s by 8000 people.

Mechanization has led to the elimination of many repetitive jobs. These days, the sugar refinery has 450 workers – with an average length of service of twenty-seven years – and makes about half a million tonnes of sugar a year. Another 300 office and support staff work across the two sites.

Those in the main control room monitor the manufacturing process on twenty consoles set up in a crescent shape.

At high tide, ships from locations including Fiji and Brazil each deliver 25,000–40,000 tonnes of raw cane sugar, which has been boiled into rough brown crystals. The crystals are scooped off the ship and transferred to the raw storage shed by long conveyor belts that end at roof level, and then the sugar pours down to form a colossal, 60,000-tonne sugar mountain.

Down the road at the syrup factory, cans and plastic bottles carrying the original image of Samson's 'lion and bees', from the Old Testament story, are whizzed overhead along channels before being filled with syrup.

At both sites, there is a strong, sweet scent in the air – a constant reminder of the product. 'The biggest challenge for these sites is the regeneration going on around us', says Gerald Mason, senior vice president of Tate & Lyle Sugars. Developers are building apartments and more housing estates nearby. Residential development does not always sit comfortably with noisy, busy factories.

However, Tate & Lyle has no plans to relocate, because it would be too costly to rebuild elsewhere. What's more, as Mason points out, 'The skills are here, so we'll be here for decades to come.'

Packaging machines for the little blue-and-white sugar bags were installed in the late 1980s and can fill two bags a second. This mound of raw sugar (centre left) has arrived by ship to be refined.

The Victorian-era design on Lyle's packaging has hardly changed since Golden Syrup was first produced in tins in 1885, although the syrup was sold in strong cardboard during the First World War, when some metal was in short supply.

Meantime Brewing
Beer

North Greenwich
meantimebrewing.com

London's pioneering craft beer business started selling its first brew, Union Lager, in 2000. Today it produces around twenty-one million pints a year.

While Alastair Hook was working at a summer camp in the United States, he became aware of the country's modern craft beer revolution. On returning home, he switched degrees to study brewing at Heriot-Watt University in Edinburgh.

Born and raised in Greenwich, Hook has located forty-strong Meantime on an industrial estate near the O2, close to the banks of the Thames. It is neighbours with the London factory of Alcatel Submarine Networks, which produces undersea telecommunications equipment.

On the forecourt stand nine large, vertical metal cylinders. Each of these maturation vessels stores and ages 90,000 pints of beer at a time.

Inside, Lee Cash, a senior brewer who has been with Meantime since the beginning, works with the other nineteen employees in production. The main piece of brewing equipment, which comes from Germany and cost £7 million, brews 17,000 pints per batch. The room also holds fifty big conical-bottomed stainless-steel vessels known as DPVs (dual-purpose vessels); these are used to both ferment and mature the beer throughout the brewing process. Once kegs are sterilized and filled, a robotic arm carries them off the conveyor, and caps and labels them before placing them on to pallets. Similarly, the mechanized bottling line labels, fills and packs bottles into boxes. Canning is handled by a sister brewery.

Cash and the team mill malted barley, turning it into a mash with hot water. That process produces a sugary substance, which is boiled up with hops for bitterness and

aroma. The liquid is cooled and yeast is added; the yeast ferments the sugar and turns it into alcohol.

The beer is then matured, sitting in cool temperatures for up to six weeks. The next step is sterile filtration to remove impurities without affecting the taste, before the beer is packaged into bottles, cans or kegs.

There are now around 150 craft breweries in the capital, according to Buddy Steiner-Lawson, general manager of Meantime's visitor centre. 'London is our home market', he says. 'Eighty per cent of our output is sold in the city, and being here gives us a close connection with consumers.'

Meantime Brewing became part of the Japanese alcoholic beverages, soft drinks and food business Asahi Group Holdings in 2016.

The ambition is to refurbish the site and increase Meantime's canned beer capacity by introducing a canning line in-house.

Founder Alastair Hook took out a second mortgage on his flat and received help from friends in order to set up Meantime Brewing in 1999. The company's first beer, Union Lager, went on sale in the following year.

Eric Mave, former packaging operator, stands outside the building in Blackwall Lane, North Greenwich.

Meantime has restarted its tours, which involve a visit to the brewhouse, the fermentation and maturation areas and the bottling line, followed by a tutored tasting session.

Time is essential to
Meantime's beers, says
Alastair Hook, who spent
four years studying brewing.
'The beer will tell you when
it's ready; you don't tell
the beer.'

Growing Underground
Salad

Clapham
growing-underground.com

In old Second World War air-raid shelters 33 metres (108 ft) under the streets of Clapham, salad leaves are being harvested. They are grown year-round in what is called a controlled-environment farm. This one uses a hydroponic system (which requires 70 per cent less water than traditional open-field farming), LED lighting and no pesticides, and is powered by 100 per cent renewable energy.

After the 2008 financial crash brought his garden-furniture business to a halt, Richard Ballard moved to London and took a degree in film. The two films he made on the history of underground London and how to feed cities in the future led him to learn more about vertical farming. 'Then I realized the benefits', he says, citing food security and the reduction of food miles.

Zero Carbon Farms, which started operating in 2016, sees itself as an agtech company, and

brands its produce Growing Underground. 'There are other people doing vertical farming in London, but most are small start-ups', explains Ballard. The thirty-five-strong team specializes in microgreens and young salad crops, which contain up to ninety times more nutrients than when they are fully grown, according to Growing Underground.

Before Ballard and his former business partner Steven Dring came along, the air-raid shelters served as temporary accommodation for post-war Caribbean migrants who arrived on the *Empire Windrush*, and were more recently rented out for document storage. They have proved to be an excellent all-year-round growing environment. Plus, 'they're an ideal location for us, as they're less than a mile from New Covent Garden Market'. The shelters are accessed via a door off Clapham High Street. Visitors go down the stairs or in the lift to long tunnels like those built for the Tube.

London's nine million inhabitants, plus its commuters, make the city 'a country in itself', says Ballard. 'You've got the consumer to take the product.' The salad goes to retailers, including Marks & Spencer, Waitrose, Ocado, Tesco and Whole Foods Market. And via food-service distribution partners at New Covent Garden Market, the business supplies cafes and restaurants across the capital.

Clapham will remain a key growing space because, as Ballard points out, 'Clapham is our USP. And it's energy-efficient, because it's a naturally controlled environment.' But it is not very accessible for packing, so much of that process is set to move to north London, to an existing warehouse on an industrial estate with better access for vehicles. This second site will allow crops to be shipped out of town more easily. 'We have the ability to produce 70 tonnes of salad leaves a year at Clapham', says Ballard. 'That will increase eight times with the new site.'

Growing Underground sows salad leaves and microgreens – vegetables such as broccoli and radish that are harvested when they are still seedlings.

Co-founder and chief operating officer Richard Ballard says Growing Underground was the first controlled-environment farm in the UK.

Instead of sitting in soil, the crops are grown on substrate made from recycled wool-rich carpet offcuts that would otherwise go to landfill.

Trays of seeds germinate under LED lights. Then they are moved to the 'farm' area, and between one and three weeks later they are picked and packed.

MATERIALS

George Jackson
Decorative plasterwork

Sutton
georgejackson.com

Before John Jackson – son of founder George Jackson – introduced fibrous plaster to the UK, making decorative plasterwork was a slow process. Cornices and other fancy elements were made on site by throwing plaster at a wall or ceiling and running a profile along it. 'It was very time-consuming', says David Serra, co-director of George Jackson.

In contrast, fibrous plaster – plaster of Paris reinforced with layers of hessian – is handled in a factory. 'You make a model, then you make a mould, then you make casts and take them to site and install them', Serra explains.

John Jackson perfected the process through trial and error. 'We believe that he researched different mould-making techniques', says Serra. George Jackson's 11,000 moulds make up one of the largest collections in the world.

In the first quarter of the twentieth century, over half of all ships were built in British shipyards, and the firm's fibrous plaster transformed the interiors of ocean liners, including the *Mauretania*, *Lusitania* and *Queen Mary*. More recently, George Jackson has created arches, columns and ceiling centrepieces and roses, as well as cornices, for Buckingham Palace, The Ritz, SS *Great Britain*, Café Royal on Regent Street, and Chelsea Barracks.

Jackson's first workshop was just north of Soho, but the business has been on a Sutton trading estate since 2007. It is the biggest decorative plasterer in the capital. 'We're in London for historical reasons, but also because most of our work is here and, being nearby, we can deal with changes very easily', says Serra.

Inside the unassuming low-rise shed, unique patterns are on display on the ground floor, alongside beautiful pieces of

David Serra has been director of George Jackson since 2011. The company designs, manufactures and installs specialist plasterwork.

plasterwork. Staff dressed in white work at long benches, while the floor is dusted white from the plaster. An internal window in the first-floor meeting area looks on to the workshop below.

At any one time, the twenty-strong firm is involved in around twenty projects. 'Most of our work is in making the models and moulds', says Serra. 'The casts are reasonably quick to make.'

Serra points out that 'although we've got a fantastic history dating back to 1780, we're about the craftspeople', and the firm trains apprentices to keep the trade alive. One of Serra's challenges is 'to bring more young people into our industry, but there's a desire for a desk job'. However, 'the pay is good, the work we do here is very interesting, and it's different every day'. Today George Jackson is a family-owned and family-managed business led by Serra and co-director Xana Haley. Their focus is on continuing the company's commitment to delivering beautifully detailed plasterwork for its customers.

The firm's vast collection of historical models and moulds is used by architects and interior designers as a source of inspiration.

The craftsmanship shows
in the sharp finishes and
detailing of the plasterwork.

'We're busier than ever', says David Serra, explaining that the business has a lot of work in high-end residential projects, mostly in London and the south-east.

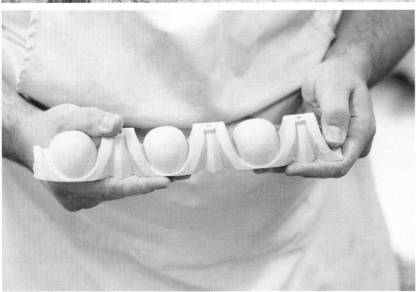

Freya Bramble-Carter and Chris Bramble
Ceramics

West Hampstead
freyabramblecarter.com / chrisbrambleceramics.com

Kingsgate Workshops is an old Victorian curtain factory full of affordable studio space rented to a tight community of artists and designer-makers. 'Some people have been in here longer than I've been alive', says Freya Bramble-Carter, who was born in 1991. 'It's a very special place. I spend more time here than anywhere else.' Inside, she and her father, Chris Bramble, each have a studio where they make ceramics and run pottery classes.

Chris, whose parents were from British Guiana, studied ceramics at Glasgow School of Art, stayed in the city for ten years and was then exhibitions officer at the National Gallery of Zimbabwe in Harare in the mid-1980s. He returned to Scotland, but the pieces he made were going to London galleries, so he moved down to where the action was, and joined Kingsgate Workshops the year Freya was born. 'The footfall is better in London than elsewhere in the UK, and there are a lot of galleries here, so it's easy to deliver to them rather than post ceramics', Chris says. What's more, 'London is an inspiring place, it's got the buzz.'

Freya grew up around clay, as both her parents were ceramicists. During her fine arts degree at Chelsea College of Arts, she connected best with the ceramics course. Her ground-floor studio has pottery wheels, a kiln and many shelves of her homeware, such as plates and bowls, and sculptural pieces for the home and garden. Some of these pieces are sold through the New Craftsmen showroom in Mayfair.

Chris, meanwhile, is known for his combination work: big simple pots with sculptural, figurative elements such as women's heads. His decades of training mean that a pot is thrown in a few minutes, but head-sculpting can take twelve hours. Father and daughter collaborate for craft shows, such as for the RHS Chelsea Flower Show in 2021.

Teaching is a key part of the Brambles' practice, and this happens upstairs, in Chris's bigger studio, where the shelves are full of his and his students' ongoing work.

Freya gets a lot out of teaching: 'Because I've had so many shows to prepare for this year, I've had months out when I haven't taught. But I've found that the magic in all this is being able to share this gift and pass the knowledge around.'

Freya Bramble-Carter makes limited-edition pieces and homeware, all of which have a strong connection to the natural world.

Ceramicist Chris Bramble handcrafts pots and sculptures inspired by his interest in the European sculptural tradition and his love of African craftsmanship, shape and form.

Father and daughter
are keen to impart their
knowledge and often have
a couple of apprentices
each. 'We're really open
to training people up',
Freya says.

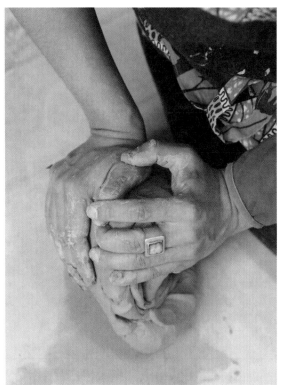

Chris and Freya run classes in Chris's studio, which has ten wheels and five kilns. Chris creates his own work alongside the students, and they learn by watching him.

Diespeker & Co.
Terrazzo and natural stone

Bermondsey
diespeker.co.uk

Terrazzo, which originated in sixteenth-century Italy, is made of marble, quartz, granite, ceramic or glass chippings set into a cement or resin binder. It is either poured *in situ* or precast into blocks, to make flooring, wall tiles, worktops, reception desks and furniture. At Diespeker & Co., it is even turned into fountains, fireplaces and plinths.

Diespeker's story starts with Luigi Odorico, an Italian entrepreneur who owned a mosaic and terrazzo company in Frankfurt. In 1881 he sent his sales rep Sigmund Diespeker and craftsman Giovanni Mariutto to England to research the potential for selling marble and terrazzo products. But instead of reporting back, the pair started Diespeker & Co. at Holborn Viaduct and became one of the first companies to offer terrazzo and mosaic in this country. Later, Mariutto took sole ownership of the company but kept the name.

Around 80 per cent of Diespeker's output is terrazzo, the rest is cut natural stone, such as marble. 'Terrazzo has had such a resurgence and we've carved a niche as an expert,' says owner John Krause, 'but things change and we're currently seeing a renewed interest in marble.'

John worked part-time at the firm through school and university from the age of seventeen. His father, Bob Krause, and two business partners had bought Diespeker from Granwood Flooring in the 1970s, and John's brother and sister also worked at the company.

Diespeker is located just off the Old Kent Road. Of the forty members of staff, twenty are on the factory floor. The bespoke workshop has not changed in years. It is known as the 'green shed', and uses traditional methods to handmake terrazzo.

The other area, which processes large pieces of stone, is noisy and full of big

machinery. The cutting machine uses water jets to reduce the amount of dust created in the factory: 'much better both for our workforce and for the environment', John says.

A number of London companies supply natural stone and terrazzo, but, says John, 'No one has the range of raw stock that we have on site, which allows clients to choose a slab of material for immediate order. And there's no one making bespoke terrazzo on the scale that we do, either.'

Meanwhile, Diespeker's site is being overhauled, giving the business 'extra space and a whole new look', and in turn refreshing its commitment to operating in inner London.

John Krause is the owner of Diespeker, whose terrazzo can be found in the Barbican, the Lloyd's Building, the Victoria and Albert Museum, the Royal Academy of Arts and the revamped Battersea Power Station.

The premises in Bermondsey house a huge display of hundreds of types of terrazzo and natural stone.

For bespoke terrazzo, the client chooses an aggregate, which is combined with the resin or cement base and a dye. The mixture is poured into a mould and hand-trowelled. Once set, the surface is ground and polished.

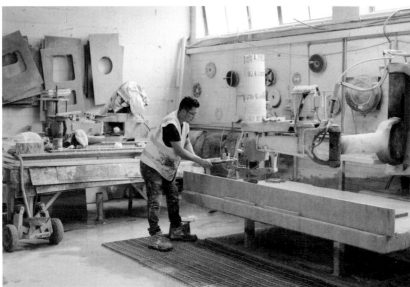

Diespeker stocks marbles such as Carrara and other stones such as granite, quartz and limestone. The chippings that are added to bespoke terrazzo mixes are also used on garden paths and driveways.

London Stone Carving
Stone carvings

Peckham
londonstonecarving.com

When four friends left the City and Guilds of London Art School clutching their diplomas in historic stone carving – the UK's only such course – 'there wasn't really anywhere that offered us the kind of work we wanted to do', says Josh Locksmith.

So in 2015 Samuel Lee, Thomas Nicholls, Tom Brown and Locksmith set up London Stone Carving to specialize in high-end, handmade stone carving. They are based off the Old Kent Road in a 1960s red-brick unit with all-important high ceilings, and lifting equipment outside. The front room is used for model-making, while 'all the mess and noise happen in the back', Locksmith says. 'There are lumps of stone and half-finished carvings dotted around, as well as drawings and plaster casts of things we've made over our career.'

Typically, stone carvers are one-man bands. But being a foursome allows them to put their portfolios together and promote a more diverse range of projects, explains Locksmith. And they can pitch themselves as a team to secure bigger jobs.

The team expected to receive commissions for a lot of architectural restoration work, such as their big Soane roses for Pitzhanger Manor in Ealing, 'but we've ended up doing art fabrication for sculptors and artists' – although they are not allowed to name names.

Apart from the invention of power tools, the process has not changed for a thousand years. First, they model a sculpture in clay or wax, then make a mould and cast the piece in plaster. 'Then it's a copying exercise, reproducing the cast in stone with a hammer and chisel and some pneumatic tools.' Nothing happens very quickly, meaning that in a year they might make six small pieces, or just one if it is large and detailed.

Being based in London is the group's selling point, and they are now in 'the nice

Co-founder and co-director Josh Locksmith is part of London Stone Carving's team of qualified masons, artists and architectural conservators.

position of being choosy' about the work they take on. In fact, the work tends to find them, often through the city's architecture and design firms. Also, 'clients want to come to the studio, because half the enjoyment for them is seeing the process', Locksmith adds.

The more mechanization and automation creep into the industry, 'the more people appreciate having something handmade', observes Locksmith.

The team's work includes replacement carvings for old churches and other historic buildings. The group also receives commissions through sculptors and artists.

People can learn the basics of stone carving on the team's courses. The lion's head (top) is one of the samples that participants make during those workshops.

Much concentration is required for the long process of chiselling detailing into the stone. In the image at bottom left, Thomas Nicholls carves a memorial for the stillbirth and neonatal death charity Sands.

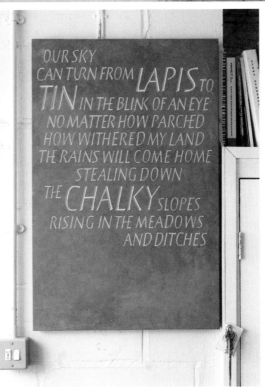

OUR SKY
CAN TURN FROM LAPIS TO
TIN IN THE BLINK OF AN EYE
NO MATTER HOW PARCHED
HOW WITHERED MY LAND
THE RAINS WILL COME HOME
STEALING DOWN
THE CHALKY SLOPES
RISING IN THE MEADOWS
AND DITCHES

Wax Atelier
Candles

Poplar
waxatelier.com

In 2017 two designer-maker friends, finding themselves in a work lull, decided to collaborate on an experimental project, and picked wax as their material. A successful product designer who sells to the New Craftsmen showroom, Lola Lely was born in Vietnam and grew up in London. Both Lely and her French-born business partner, Yesenia Thibault-Picazo – a musician as well as a designer – had taught on the material futures course at Central Saint Martins, so were used to exploring the properties of raw materials.

After making their own tools, sourcing beeswax from a beekeeper neighbour in Walthamstow, and teaching themselves to dip candles by watching YouTube videos, the two fell in love with the process and the product as a 'functional, beautiful, everyday thing', says Lely.

Initially, the duo ran workshops in Lely's studio at Blackhorse Workshop in Walthamstow. People wanted to buy the candles, and one Christmas they had so many orders that they had to call in family and friends to help make them.

Wax Atelier's candles are now stocked by over 200 retailers worldwide, many of whom like being seen to be working with authentic, creative makers. One of the first collaborations was with the fashion and homeware brand Toast. 'We don't feel as if we've strategized', says Lely. 'It's been a huge surprise.'

For several years, Wax Atelier operated out of Everyone's Warehouse in Barking, one of the UK's biggest open-access workshops, which introduces locals to making skills and supports business ideas. The area had been in decline since the 1980s, when many factories closed, and many residents had been out of work for a long time.

The company's ten staff are mostly local women, all of whom have taken part in an intensive nine-week training programme. They make 120 candles and about thirty waxed foodwraps a day. The number of candles doubles in August, in anticipation of Christmas, when staff are offered overtime and the founders jump in to help.

In 2022 Wax Atelier moved to bigger premises at Poplar Works, which has over forty studios for creative and fashion enterprises. The business plans to expand into homeware, in part through a collaboration with a craft community in north Vietnam that works with hemp, paper and beeswax.

While businesses making poured scented candles have mushroomed in recent years as part of the craft-making boom, Lely believes that Wax Atelier is the only company in London making hand-dipped candles. She adds: 'We like this ancient method.'

Co-founders Yesenia Thibault-Picazo (left) and Lola Lely in their Barking workshop, which they moved out of in 2022. The wax-splattered room smelled of warm wax and natural scents.

The vats are turned on at 8.30 am, and the wax is molten by 11 am, when the candle-makers arrive. The first dip for each candle is thirty seconds, to allow the wax to bond to the wick.

'You must dip evenly, or you will have lines, ridges and bubbles on the candle's surface. It's very meditative. We usually have music on', Lely says. Pictured above are Carina Murray (front) and Rebecca Bowker, who have been making candles for Wax Atelier since 2019.

Each maker has ten racks, and each rack holds eight candles. Wax textiles were made on the other side of the Barking studio.

Around 70 per cent of Wax Atelier's sales are wholesale, and the rest is made up of direct selling online and customers purchasing candles from the workshop.

ACKNOWLEDGEMENTS

It was a privilege to meet everyone I encountered and to see behind the scenes of so many workshops and factories during the making of this book. Some people I met had worked at the same place all their working lives, and I hope this book reflects their dedication and skill, and honours their contributions to London's vibrant manufacturing scene. The book could not have been made without Mark Brearley's extensive knowledge and years of research. It has been a pleasure to collaborate with him and to create a book that demonstrates his enthusiasm and determination to keep 'the messy as well as the neat' in London. I am keen to continue documenting different regions and types of production across the British Isles, celebrating the people who make the things we use every day. Mark and I have discussed this book project ever since we met five years ago and started working together on visual audits of London's industry. We have been so fortunate to have worked with Hugh Merrell and his team, who have listened to our ideas, given us creative freedom and worked in a truly collaborative way. Thank you to Nicola Bailey for her patience and expertise and for having done a great job with the layout, and to Claire Chandler for her brilliant attention to detail when editing the book. Thanks also to Clare Dowdy, who interviewed the business-owners and wrote all the texts, capturing succinctly the history and atmosphere of each workshop or factory. I could not have thrown myself into this project without Matt keeping the show on the road at home and looking after our three young kids – all my love and thanks. My siblings and parents have provided encouragement and support when I needed them, as have Nat Harrison, Laura Bunt, Will and Annabelle Cruickshank, Steve Joyce, Bex Seal, Lucy Harvey, Alice Paling and Mark Sinclair. Debbie Bliss, Nicola Read, James Pallister and Sara Carneholm all helped with early versions of this project.
Carmel King

Finding out who manufactures in London, and building up a list of some 3600 active businesses, is the venture that prompted the making of this book. Assembling that list took me ages. I roamed the internet, walked the streets, made notes of what I saw on the sides of vans and lorries, looked at product labels, asked people and delved into various business audits. The people in businesses are nearly always friendly, and all who are drawn in share their knowledge and time freely. Thanks, then, to all who helped with the discovery process and subsequently the making of this book. They include: the team at Kaymet and friends in the Old Kent Road area; the lively people at Make UK, the Federation of Small Businesses, the Royal Warrant Holders Association, the Centre for London and Open City; my colleagues at the School of Art, Architecture and Design at London Metropolitan University (and thanks to that institution for supporting this as a research project); various companions on my exploratory walks, including Ivana Milanovic, the Brearley sisters, Jan Zaman, Ellis Woodman, Julian Lewis, Graeme Sutherland and Tom Young; all those in the businesses that I talked to or visited. I thank everyone else who has encouraged me in this effort, including my family and my brother; collaborators elsewhere in Europe, such as Mr Zaman, Roeland Dudal and others in Brussels; the incomparable Professor Peter Carl; Peter Murray (whose 'Blessed are the traymakers' headline cheered me on); and several from much-missed Design for London. It has been a pleasure working with Clare Dowdy and with Hugh Merrell and his publishing team; hats off to Merrell for taking a chance on this book and being so determined to make it excellent. And I salute Carmel King's endless energy, great skill, and passion for celebrating the daily achievements of producers.
Mark Brearley

AUTHOR BIOGRAPHIES

PICTURE CREDITS

CARMEL KING is a photographer who has spent more than a decade documenting craftspeople, heritage brands and independent businesses across the British Isles. Inspired by her own family's three-generation textile firm, she is passionate about capturing traditional crafts and celebrating the best of British making and industry.

carmelking.com

MARK BREARLEY is an architect and urbanist with special expertise in urban industry and its future. He is currently Professor of Urbanism at London Metropolitan University's School of Art, Architecture and Design. Until 2013 he worked for the Mayor of London as Head of Design for London at the Greater London Authority. He is also proprietor of the long-established London tray and trolley manufacturer Kaymet, and for the past decade has been cataloguing London manufacturers.

CLARE DOWDY is a freelance journalist, editor, copywriter and curator. She has written about design, architecture and manufacturing for the *Financial Times*, *Monocle*, *Wallpaper* and BBC.com, and edited the online magazine *Furnace*, which championed factories.

How will the
global economy
heal from the
health crisis?

"If anything kills over
10 million people in the next few
decades, it's most likely to be a highly
infectious virus rather than a war."

INDEX

For Mum and Dad and all the Mortons
Carmel King

Thanks for the friendship of
Richard Rogers, who left us as
we prepared this book
Mark Brearley

First published 2022 by Merrell Publishers,
London and New York

Merrell Publishers Limited
70 Cowcross Street
London EC1M 6EJ

merrellpublishers.com

British Library Cataloguing in Publication Data.
A catalogue record for this book is available from
the British Library.

ISBN 978-1-8589-4702-0

Produced by Merrell Publishers Limited
Designed by Nicola Bailey
Project-managed by Claire Chandler
Proofread by Barbara Roby
Indexed by Hilary Bird

Printed and bound in China

NOTE ON TYPE
The titling typeface is LDN Southbank, designed by
Paul Harpin for the London Type Foundry. The foundry
creates typefaces inspired by the heritage, diversity
and creativity of London. LDN Southbank pays tribute
to the graphic designers who studied at the Royal
College of Art in the early 1950s, during the Festival
of Britain era.

londontype.co.uk

Front cover: Mario Jaramillo at work at George Jackson,
Sutton, where he has been employed since 2017; see
pp. 220–23.

Back cover: Steve Whitton and Nathan Gardner at Whitton
Castings, Woolwich; see pp. 114–17.

Frontispiece: Raw cane sugar is unloaded on Tate & Lyle's
jetty in Silvertown; see pp. 206–209.

Pages 4–5: Experienced brazers at work in Brompton's
vast factory in Greenford; see pp. 66–69.

Pages 6–7: Components of a private jet are resprayed at
JETMS Completions, Biggin Hill; see pp. 78–81.

Pages 8–9: Experienced seamstresses make military wear
at Kashket & Partners, Tottenham; see pp. 30–33.

Page 10: Some 75,000 Brompton bikes are made each year
and sold globally.

Pages 240–41: Plaster models of ceiling roses line the walls
at George Jackson.

Page 243: The power presses at William Say & Co.,
Bermondsey, range in date from the 1950s to the modern
day; see pp. 126–29.

Pages 244–45: Wheels are inspected at Brompton's
8000-square-metre (86,000 sq. ft) factory unit.

Page 247: *Pointe* shoes in production at Freed of London,
Hackney; see pp. 26–29.

Pages 248–49: Luan Qeloposhi at Richmond Bridge
Boathouses, Richmond upon Thames; see pp. 82–85.

Page 250: One of the huge printing presses in action
at Empress Litho in Woolwich; see pp. 176–79.

Overleaf: Robert Bent on the factory floor at BIZ Karts,
Brimsdown, where he has worked since 1998; see pp. 74–77.

CHAPTER OPENERS
Pages 20–21: Blackhorse Lane Ateliers (see pp. 22–25);
pages 42–43: Jost Haas (see pp. 56–59); pages 64–65:
BIZ Karts (see pp. 74–77); pages 86–87: Aimer Products
(see pp. 100–103); pages 108–109: Whitton Castings
(see pp. 114–17); pages 130–31: Marcus Hall Props (see
pp. 140–43); pages 152–53: Savoir Beds (see pp. 158–61);
pages 174–75: Ivo Prints (see pp. 192–95); pages 196–97:
Tate & Lyle Sugars (see pp. 206–209); pages 218–19:
George Jackson (see pp. 220–23).